THE M. & E. HANDBOOK SERIES
CLERICAL DUTIES

THE M. & E. HANDBOOK SERIES

CLERICAL DUTIES

J. C. DENYER

A.C.I.S., A.H.A., M.Inst.A.M., A.M.B.I.M.
Senior Lecturer at South West London College

SECOND EDITION

MACDONALD & EVANS LTD
8 John Street, London WC1N 2HY

First published August 1970
Reprinted March 1972
Reprinted May 1973
Reprinted February 1974
Second edition November 1975

©

MACDONALD AND EVANS LIMITED
1975

ISBN: 0 7121 0353 8

This book is copyright and may not be reproduced in whole *or in part* (except for purposes of review) without the express permission of the publishers in writing.

HANDBOOK *Conditions of sale*
This book is sold subject to the condition that it shall not, by way of *trade or otherwise*, be lent, resold, hired out or otherwise *circulated* without the publisher's prior consent in any form of binding or cover other than that in which it is published *and without a similar condition including this condition being imposed on the subsequent purchaser.*

Filmset by Keyspools Limited
Golborne Lancs.
Printed in Great Britain by
Hazell Watson and Viney Limited
Aylesbury, Buckinghamshire

PREFACE TO THE SECOND EDITION

THIS book is intended primarily for students taking the Certificate in Office Studies, but could equally well be used by any student intending to enter office life for the first time.

Following the pattern laid down by the National Committee for the award of the Certificate, the book is written to cover a two-year course of study. The first year is concerned with the commercial world, the setting in which the office operates. The second half then narrows to an examination of the activities taking place in the office.

To lend reality to much of the material, teachers are advised to prepare practical exercises for students, on such matters as writing of invoices and preparation of a pay-roll, and to give demonstrations as well as instruction in the use of simple office machines. Although illustrations of the most important documents are included in the book, it is impossible to depict every document (or variety of it) used in business, and teachers are also advised to amplify the material in the text with other specimens of business forms not included.

Self-testing examination questions are added at the end of each chapter, so that the style and content of possible examination questions can be assessed.

These questions are based on the syllabus requirements of the Certificate in Office Studies, and I wish to express my thanks to the following bodies for granting permission to quote from past examination papers:

    East Midland Education Union (E.M.E.U.)
    Northern Counties Technical Examinations Council (N.C.T.E.C.)
    Royal Society of Arts (R.S.A.)
    Union of Educational Institutions (U.E.I.)
    Union of Lancashire and Cheshire Institutes (U.L.C.I.)
    Welsh Joint Education Committee (W.J.E.C.)
    Yorkshire Council for Further Education (Y.C.F.E.)

February 1975   J.C.D

NOTICE TO LECTURERS

Many lecturers are now using **HANDBOOKS** as working texts to save time otherwise wasted by students in protracted note-taking. The purpose of the series is to meet practical teaching requirements as far as possible, and lecturers are cordially invited to forward comments or criticisms to the publishers for consideration.

P. W. D. REDMOND
General Editor

CONTENTS

CHAP.		PAGE
	Preface to the second edition	v
	List of illustrations	viii

PART ONE: THE COMMERCIAL BACKGROUND

I.	The business world	1
II.	Departments of a business	6
III.	Buying	15
IV.	Sales	24
V.	Transport	36
VI.	Stock	48
VII.	Money and banking	59
VIII.	Petty cash	74
IX.	The accountant's department	78

PART TWO: CLERICAL SERVICES

X.	The office	81
XI.	Office communications	85
XII.	Filing and records	93
XIII.	Inwards and outwards mail	107
XIV.	Typing and typing pools	119
XV.	Duplicating and photocopying	122
XVI.	Books of reference	129
XVII.	Personnel practice	134
XVIII.	Timekeeping and wages	139
XIX.	Adding, calculating and accounting machines	146
XX.	Miscellaneous office machines	153

APPENDIXES

I.	Acts of Parliament	158
II.	Examination technique	159

INDEX	163

LIST OF ILLUSTRATIONS

FIG.

1.	Organisation chart	7
2.	Requisition note	17
3.	Letter of enquiry	18
4.	Quotation	19
5.	Order	20
6.	Delivery note	30
7.	Invoice	31
8.	Statement	32
9.	Log book of petrol and oil	39
10.	Shipping note	43
11.	Freight note	44
12.	Stock record	53
13.	Stock requisition	55
14.	Cheque	63
15.	Credit transfer	67
16.	Credit transfer summary form	67
17.	Paying-in slip	71
18.	Petty-cash book	75
19.	Petty-cash voucher	77
20.	Telephone message form	89
21.	Out guide	94
22.	Cross-reference	95
23.	Columns of a post book	110
24.	Holiday rota	136

PART ONE

THE COMMERCIAL BACKGROUND

CHAPTER I

THE BUSINESS WORLD

1. Business organisation. Perhaps the first thing for a student to realise is that the function, the operation and the organisation of a concern will vary with the type of business it happens to be.

Business concerns are those which are preoccupied with making a profit, but office work is also carried on in a number of other enterprises, and a list of different areas of business activity is as follows:

(*a*) Commercial concerns carried on for a profit.

(*b*) Nationalised concerns, carried on for a profit, *e.g.* the electricity boards, and those carried on to provide a service, *e.g.* the B.B.C.

(*c*) Non-profit-making bodies such as chambers of commerce, trade unions, etc.

(*d*) Co-operative societies.

(*e*) Local authorities and the Civil Service.

(*f*) Social services, such as the National Health Service.

In **2–7** below there follows an outline of the different kinds of concern which have offices and employ office workers. The first part of this book is about the activities commonly undertaken in the spheres outlined in these sections.

2. The commercial world. The basis of English society is commerce, and, other than the categories mentioned above, the *business* world consists of the following types of business concern:

(*a*) *Trading concerns.* Trading is one of the oldest business activities, and is another name for buying and selling, and making a profit in the process. There are various kinds of business unit, but they all have one thing in common—they buy goods and sell goods, although with some there may be manufacturing in between. Those who sell commodities in the same form as they buy them are called *retailers*; those who have a factory and manufacture the goods they sell are called *manufacturers*; and in some instances, where only bulk goods are sold to retailers, the sellers may be called *wholesalers*.

There is nothing wrong in making a profit, for, unless sufficient profit is made, a business will have to cease its activities and it will disappear from existence.

(*b*) *Banking concerns.* These assist the business world by providing safe-keeping of money, providing easy means of payment (*e.g.* by cheque) and on occasions lending money to a business which is short of capital.

(*c*) *Insurance concerns.* These offer compensation for loss due to fire, burglary, etc., and are a very important part of the business world.

(*d*) *Transport concerns.* These provide means of transporting goods from one place to another, by road, rail, sea or air, and can be of great service to a business which cannot afford to supply its own transport.

(*e*) *Warehousing concerns.* These provide storage of goods (often at the docks and airport) until the trader wishes to take delivery of them.

(*f*) *Financial concerns.* These mostly provide traders with facilities for borrowing finance or capital. These loans may be either long term or to assist an importer or exporter for a short period only.

NOTE: While (*a*) is concerned with the buying and selling of *goods*, (*b*) to (*f*) are engaged in selling *services*.

This outline of trading concerns includes transport, which is partly nationalised (British Rail, etc.), and warehousing, which may be provided by a public authority.

3. Nationalised concerns. Gas, coal, electricity and atomic power are examples of businesses run by the state. They are still businesses which operate for a profit, but their function is also to provide a service to the community. One of the major ways in which nationalised concerns differ from ordinary business concerns is that they often have a monopoly in their trade. This means that no other concern is allowed to sell gas or electricity, for example. It must not be thought, however, that nationalised concerns alone have a monopoly in their trade, for some private businesses also have a monopoly or near-monopoly in the supply of their products.

As stated above, some of the nationalised concerns do not sell products like a business, but supply a service—such as the B.B.C. Commercial television, on the other hand, is run by private business concerns under licence from the Government.

4. Non-profit-making bodies. For various reasons, some organisations are set up whose main purpose may be the pursuit of some artistic, sporting, educational or political aim. They of course need money to carry on their activities, and usually their activities are supported by annual subscriptions paid by members of the body concerned.

A good example of such bodies are the professional bodies founded for the furtherance of the professional interest of their members, such as the Institute of Chartered Secretaries and Administrators.

5. Co-operative societies. These businesses are run for the purpose of making profit, but their aim is that the customers should be the owners of the business and share the profit among them. This form of business is the opposite of ordinary businesses which make profit for the owner or owners of the enterprise, although in so far as the customers are the shareholders they are also the owners.

6. Local authorities and the Civil Service. The local authorities and the Civil Service in the main provide services for the community, the money for which comes from the community in the form of rates and taxes. The services they provide are those such as education, housing, roads, etc.

7. Social services. Distinct from local authorities and the Civil Service, and yet similar in many ways, are the social services. Bodies such as the National Health Service, Department of Health and Social Security, etc., provide services for the community such as medical care, National Insurance, etc., which are financed mostly by taxes paid by everyone.

8. Types of business unit. There are many forms of business unit in existence, varying from the "one-man" business to a large-scale public company like Marks and Spencer Ltd., which has over 20,000 employees.

The following are the main types:

(a) Sole trader (a "one-man" business). This type of unit exists where the business is owned and run by *one man* who performs all the business functions of buying, selling, keeping accounts, etc. It is ideally suited where a personal service is performed, such as watch-repairing, shoe-repairing, etc.

(b) Partnerships. These exist where two or more persons run a business together with a view to sharing profits between them. More capital is thus available for expansion, and the experience of the different partners can contribute to the improvement and expansion of the joint enterprise. This type of unit is also useful if one partner is absent, as the others can deputise for him; it is thus very suitable for solicitors, doctors, etc.

(c) Private companies. A company is a form of enterprise where the owners are shareholders of the company, and a private company is intended for the family concern and is distinguished by the following characteristics:

 (*i*) There is a restriction on the company's right to transfer its shares (*i.e.* perhaps to keep the shares inside the family).
 (*ii*) The company is prohibited from issuing its shares to the public.
 (*iii*) The company limits the number of its shareholders to fifty.

(d) Public companies. These are companies which issue shares to the public, and anybody can thus become a shareholder in such a company. It is a useful form of business unit when a company wishes to expand and is short of capital, for it can then issue shares to the public.

NOTE

 (*i*) *Limited liability.* Both private and public companies have "limited liability," which means that the liability of the shareholders is limited to the amount of the shares held. For example, if a sole trader runs his business badly and gets into debt, his private possessions can be seized for paying the debts of the business, but, if his business grows in size and he subsequently forms a company, all that he can then lose is his shares in the company.

(ii) *Registered office*. Every company must state in the Memorandum of Association which it files with the Registrar of Companies the name and address of its registered office, which is the company's official address. Outside the premises which it names, it must clearly display that it is the registered office of the company.

(iii) *Board of directors*. Since it is not possible for thousands of shareholders to run a company, the shareholders elect directors to control the company's affairs on their behalf. In private companies, of course, the directors are usually also the main shareholders, but in public companies the shareholders elect the directors at the annual general meeting.

(e) *Public corporations*. These are those bodies run as a business in the public interest, such as the electricity and gas boards, British Airways, the B.B.C., etc.

The managing bodies of such corporations are rather similar to the boards of directors of companies, except that they are usually appointed by the Government, and have the duty of running their enterprises in the public interest rather than in the interest of shareholders.

PROGRESS TEST 1

1. Explain the terms (a) board of directors, (b) partnership, (c) limited company, (d) registered office, (e) company secretary. (**8**)

[*U.L.C.I.*

2. How different is a private limited company from a co-operative society? (**5, 8**)

3. What kinds of business would be suitable for (a) a sole trader, (b) a partnership and (c) a private company? (**8**)

4. Name and describe the importance of five kinds of commercial enterprise. (**8**)

NOTE: The questions not followed by initials of examining bodies are suggested questions only.

CHAPTER II

DEPARTMENTS OF A BUSINESS

1. Organisation. There is nothing standard about the organisation of a business, although if it is involved in trading (*i.e.* buying and selling) it is almost certain to have both buying and selling departments. But, the larger a business grows, the more complicated does its organisation become, and the more likely is it to have departments peculiar to its own requirements. Thus, a large concern may have an export department (or division), a welfare officer and a separate training officer.

All that can be done is to gain some idea of the most usual departments found in business, as well as their most usual functions. But, in practice, the functions of any department may also vary from one concern to another. Thus, a personnel officer in one concern may be more occupied with negotiating with trade unions, while in another concern with the recruiting and training of staff.

The departments found in an enterprise will also vary with the type of enterprise. Thus a manufacturing concern (having a factory) will most probably have a production control department and a works manager, which will not be found in a business concerned solely with trading, nor in a government office.

The main departments and personnel which should be known are as follows:

    (*a*) Company secretary: *see* **2** below.
    (*b*) Accountant (including cost accountant and cashier): *see* **3** below.
    (*c*) Sales manager: *see* **4** below.
    (*d*) Purchasing (or buying): *see* **5** below.
    (*e*) Personnel (and welfare): *see* **6** below.
    (*f*) Works or production department: *see* **7** below.

In addition, some knowledge of how they relate to one another is also necessary.

A typical organisation chart of a medium-sized manufacturing company might be as shown in Fig. 1:

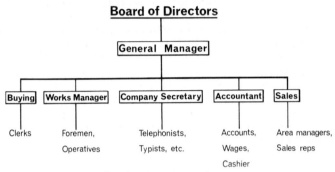

FIG. 1.—*Organisation chart.*

2. Company secretary. Every registered company must have a company secretary by law, and his duties will vary from one business to another, but generally speaking his duties are as follows:

(*a*) *General office administration.* This involves his being in charge of typing, mail, messenger and telephone services, and possibly the appointment of clerical staff.

Part of the company secretary's responsibility extends to the following:

(*i*) *Reception.* This is concerned with the receiving of callers at the business premises and passing them to the appropriate department concerned with their particular business.

(*ii*) *Registry.* The registry deals with filing, but sometimes this is also the task of the central mailing section. These departments are placed together, because incoming letters are usually matched with the relevant correspondence file, and copies of outgoing letters have also to be placed on the relevant files. With such a department, the filing and mail services are provided centrally for all departments.

NOTE: An *office manager* is often appointed in large business concerns to assist the company secretary in the general office administration. This is because of the growing complexity of office management today, which is concerned with office systems, office machines, staffing, telephones, maintenance of machines, ventilation, etc.

(b) *Statutory books and returns.* The company's secretary is made responsible under the *Companies Act* 1967 for the keeping of certain statutory books (such as the Register of Members, *i.e.* shareholders), as well as for making special statutory returns to the Registrar of Companies.

In large companies, there is a registrar's department which keeps the share register and deals with transfers of shares, etc.

(c) *Meetings.* The company secretary is responsible for all duties in connection with meetings of the directors and of shareholders, and has to arrange for the meetings, prepare agenda papers and minutes, and, more important still, see that appropriate action is taken on the decisions made at these meetings.

3. Accountant. The accountant of a business (sometimes called the "chief accountant") has the following main functions:

(a) He keeps books of account relating to the financial affairs of the business.

(b) He is responsible for the preparation of annual accounts, which are presented to the shareholders at the annual general meeting.

(c) He is in charge of the cash of the business and the bank account.

(d) He prepares and pays wages and salaries.

(e) He maintains the stock records.

(f) He pays the creditors of the business, and also collects cash from its debtors.

(g) He is responsible for sales invoicing to the customers of the business for all the goods sold.

(h) He deals with the tax liability of the business.

Costing. In a manufacturing concern, the accountant, or possibly a separate cost accountant, will be concerned with analysing the costs of production, per product or per contract. The main aims of costing are to give better financial control over detailed costs, with the purpose of improving the efficiency and ultimately increasing the profit of the business.

Cashier. The cashier is usually under the control of the accountant, and his job is the receipt and payment of all money on behalf of the business and the keeping of proper records thereof. He will deal with the company's bank account, as well as actual cash for wages and petty cash and postage.

4. Sales manager. The functions of the sales manager and, under him, the sales department are as follows:

(*a*) To decide what the customers want to buy (*i.e.* to assess the market).

(*b*) To see if such products can be made or are in fact already made.

(*c*) To let possible purchasers know of the product.

(*d*) To persuade them to buy the goods being sold (advertising, etc.).

(*e*) To deliver the goods to them (transport).

(*f*) To keep records so that control can be exercised over sales to individual customers, as well as control over sales representatives selling the company's goods.

In connection with the above, a sales manager will advise on policy regarding selling prices, remuneration of salesmen, and media of advertising, etc.

NOTE: In some businesses, the sales manager is called the "sales director"; *i.e.* he is a company director as well as being in charge of sales.

5. Purchasing (buying, procuring of supplies). This department is concerned with buying all the goods required by the business, which will include raw materials (for a factory), manufactured goods, machines, stationery, office furniture, etc. More specifically, the job of the purchasing department is as follows:

(*a*) To purchase the right goods required by the different users in the concern.

(*b*) To purchase the right quantities of goods.

(*c*) To purchase at the right time, and for delivery at the right time.

(*d*) To purchase at the right price.

(*e*) To use the best methods of purchasing.

(*f*) Probably to be in charge of stores where the goods are stocked.

(*g*) To certify on purchase invoices that goods have been received.

(*h*) To carry out testing procedures to ensure that the goods bought are of the right quality.

6. Personnel (staff office or establishment office). There are no standard duties which belong to a <u>personnel department</u>, and, while the functions usually include welfare and training, in larger business concerns there may be in addition a separate welfare officer and a separate training officer.

However, the usual duties of a <u>personnel officer</u> can be summarised as follows:

(*a*) <u>Recruitment of staff</u> (advertising, interviewing, etc.).
(*b*) <u>Education and training of staff</u>.
(*c*) <u>Working conditions and safety</u>.
(*d*) <u>Industrial relations,</u> particularly negotiating with trade unions on <u>hours of work</u> and <u>rates of pay</u>, etc.
(*e*) <u>Employee services and welfare</u>.
(*f*) Keeping staff records and staff reports.
(*g*) Settling internal disputes and dealing with discipline, promotions and transfers of staff from one department to another.

Welfare officer. Where there *is* a separate official, he is concerned with the <u>working conditions</u> and with seeing that the legal requirements are obeyed, with the <u>canteen</u>, <u>sports and recreational facilities</u>, with the <u>cloakrooms</u> and <u>washing facilities</u>; and in some concerns he helps employees with <u>personal problems</u> relating to <u>housing</u>, <u>education</u>, etc.

Training officer. Again, where there *is* a separate official (as with the welfare officer, his duties in some concerns are dealt with by the personnel officer), he is concerned with assessing what training is needed for the whole of the staff of the business and with making arrangements for various kinds of training. He is responsible for <u>assessing the adequacy of the arrangements</u>, for <u>keeping individual records of personnel undergoing training</u>, and for <u>submitting reports to management</u> on the success of arrangements made, as well as on costs.

The personnel department. This department is generally a part of management, and its main aim can be said to be <u>to recruit the best staff</u>, to see that the best use is made of them when employed, and, when good staff are recruited, to try to ensure <u>that they stay in the business</u>.

One of the methods used to assess the <u>satisfaction of the staff</u>

in the jobs they are doing is to measure labour turnover, or the ratio of staff leaving to the total number of staff employed, usually expressed as a percentage and taken over a fixed period of time, say twelve months.

Personnel thus supplies a very important service to management, but, in so far as it is concerned with the training and welfare of staff, it is also very important to the workers. Although sensational strikes are reported in the newspapers, no mention is made of the strikes averted by the personnel officer and his negotiations with shop stewards or with trade unions. In this way, he assists management and workers simultaneously.

As an example of the work done in connection with the recruitment of staff, a departmental head wanting a new member of staff will put in a request to the personnel department (which must be justified if it is for an addition to the staff), and will give information about the job to be done, the skills required, and the age, sex, and education required for the job.

7. Works manager. In a manufacturing business, the works manager (sometimes called the "production manager") has the following duties:

(*a*) He is responsible for *overall supervision of the factory*. His duties here will include the planning of production to see that the right goods are manufactured in the right time, and in accordance with specification. He will (in conjunction with the personnel officer) arrange for the training of operatives and foremen.

(*b*) He will *plan new methods of production* and recommend the purchase or replacement of factory machines.

(*c*) He will (in conjunction with the personnel officer or even with a special safety officer) *organise safety campaigns* in the works.

(*d*) He will (in conjunction with the purchasing officer) ensure that supplies of *raw materials* are delivered in time for manufacturing to take place.

(*e*) In conjunction with the welfare officer, he will be concerned with the provision of *good working conditions*, to see that there is adequate lighting, heating and ventilation.

(*f*) In conjunction with the accountant or the cost accountant, he will keep records of *costs of manufacturing* and may have to keep within a *budget* laid down for direct costs of manufacturing.

R & D (*research and development*). In smaller concerns, this may be referred to merely as the "drawing office", although in large concerns the drawing office may be distinct from the R & D department proper. The purpose of research and development is to discover new materials, new methods, or even entirely new products (thus nylon and terylene were discovered in the R & D laboratories of big textile manufacturers). It is a very important department because the whole progress of the business may depend on the outcome of proper research.

Stock department (*or stores*). This department keeps stocks of goods. The *stores* department usually keeps tools, raw materials, etc., while the *stock* department usually keeps the stocks of finished goods which have been manufactured and are waiting to be sold.

The stock department has to keep securely all the stock entrusted to it and issue the goods only on the production of proper documents of authorisation. In addition it must keep detailed stock records, showing goods received and issued, and the balance of any item still in hand.

The stock department usually comes under the supervision of the works manager, but in some concerns it is managed by the company's buyer.

8. Inter-relationship of departments. It can be seen from what has been mentioned that all departments of a business are related to one another, and to emphasise this aspect the following might be observed:

(*a*) *The accountant's department* is related to all other departments, because it is concerned with costs of buying materials (buying department), with costs of production (works manager), with costs of labour (personnel department) and so on.

(*b*) *The personnel department* is also related to all other departments because it is concerned with the recruitment and training of staff, and the assessment of labour turnover in all departments.

(*c*) *The sales department* is related to the production department, because in a manufacturing business the sales staff will have knowledge of what customers are buying and therefore what should be manufactured. The sales department will also be closely related to the stock and to the transport departments, because it must ensure that there are sufficient stocks of goods to supply to customers, and it must also be aware of the delivery periods for specific goods, so that it can quote delivery periods to customers.

9. Conclusion. Only a brief outline of the work of these main departments of a business has been given, and fuller details and an outline of the forms and systems used are given in subsequent chapters.

PROGRESS TEST 2

1. Describe the departmental layout of a large modern organisation, and show by means of a chart how the various duties are allocated. (**1**) [*W.J.E.C.*

2. Name *four* departments found in a large business organisation. (**1**) [*W.J.E.C.*

3. You are employed by a light engineering firm which has doubled in size in the last two years and which finds its administrative system no longer adequate for its needs.
You are asked (*a*) to draw up a simple organisation chart showing the different departments into which you think the business could be divided, and (*b*) to state clearly and precisely for which aspects of the work of the business you think each department should be responsible. (**2**) [*R.S.A.*

4. What is a reception register? Draft the headings of such a register and make one entry. (**2**) [*U.L.C.I.*

5. Write brief explanatory notes (*inter alia*) on the company secretary. (**2**) [*Y.C.F.E.*

6. What work is performed by a central correspondence and filing section or registry? (**2**) [*N.C.T.E.C.*

7. Describe the work of a cashier's department in an office. (**3**) [*U.L.C.I.*

8. Your general manager has called a meeting of heads of department and among those present are the works manager, sales manager, purchasing manager and chief accountant.

(*a*) Outline the main responsibilities of each of these executives.

(*b*) Indicate the close relationship which must exist between any *two* of them in an efficient organisation. (**3**–**7**) [*R.S.A.*

9. Describe *two* of the following divisions of the office: (*a*) purchasing, (*b*) stock, (*c*) staff and personnel, (*d*) costing. (**3, 5, 6, 7**) [*N.C.T.E.C.*

10. Describe *two* of the following divisions of the office: (*a*) staff and personnel, (*b*) cashier's department, (*c*) planning and research. (**3, 6, 7**) [*N.C.T.E.C.*

11. What are the functions of the sales section in an office? (**4**)
[*U.L.C.I.*

12. You are a member of the personnel department of a large industrial organisation. What information would you want the head of another department to give you to find him a new employee? (**6**)
[*R.S.A.*

13. What are the functions of the staff and personnel section in an office? (**6**) [*U.L.C.I.*

14. What are the duties of a welfare officer in a large business? (**6**)
[*Y.C.F.E.*

15. Describe the work of a personnel manager. In your answer refer to the services he provides (*a*) for management and (*b*) for employees. (**6**) [*Y.C.F.E.*

16. What are the relations of a personnel department in connection with staff welfare and staff turnover? (**6**) [*N.C.T.E.C.*

17. Why are good staff welfare facilities necessary and important? (**6**) [*U.L.C.I.*

18. Describe the work of any *one* business department of your choice. [*U.L.C.I.*

19. Write an account of the work of any one department in an office. In your answer illustrate how three different types of work are used to improve efficiency. [*E.M.E.U.*

CHAPTER III

BUYING

1. Organisation of the department. The organisation of a buying department will vary according to the size of the business. Thus, in a small business, one person may be responsible for all the buying, but in a large business concern there will be a buying manager (or puchasing officer or supplies officer) who is in charge of the department and who will exercise general control over all the office staff (each of whom will usually buy specific goods), liaise with the company accountant, sales manager and personnel officer, as well as deal with all work problems and assist in the recruitment and training of his own staff. He will be the expert who will advise management on buying policy, and will deal personally with important contracts, etc.

The buying manager's staff is usually divided into the following:

(a) Order clerks.

(b) Follow-up clerks (*i.e.* if each order clerk does not perform his own follow-up). This is an important aspect of the work, being the frequent enquiring after goods which have not been delivered by the promised dates.

(c) Typing and filing clerks.

2. Methods of buying. Part of the responsibility of the buying manager is to decide on the policies to be followed when buying goods, and while the quotation method is the most popular it is not the only method. There are four main methods of buying, and the procedures and forms used will vary according to the method used.

(a) *Spot purchase.* This is where goods are bought on the spot either at an outside showroom or warehouse, or over the telephone, or from a sales representative visiting the office. This method is used for items of small value, or where there may be only one supplier, or where the company has dealt satisfactorily with a certain supplier for many years.

The sales representative of the supplier is asked about the price and availability of the goods required, and, if this information is satisfactory, an official order is written out and given or sent through the post straight away.

(b) *By quotation.* By this method several printed forms of quotation may be sent to different suppliers asking them to quote prices for specified goods (a sample of what is required may be supplied to them), after which their qualities are compared and the order given to the one which quotes the most favourable terms. This is dealt with in more detail in **5** below.

(c) *By contract.* This is where a long-term contract is negotiated with a specified supplier (often negotiated by the buying manager) for (say) a year's supply of a certain commodity at a specified price, and deliveries may be had as required during the year. This method is used where large quantities of (say) raw materials are required, and it has the advantage of buying at a very low price because of the total quantity of the order.

(d) *By tender.* This is a method mostly used by public bodies where advertisements in newspapers or trade journals invite suppliers to tender their prices for certain commodities on the basis of which contracts are awarded to the most favourable tenderers ("tender" means an offer; the supplier is offering to supply the goods required).

3. Categories of goods purchased. There can be no standard classification of goods purchased, because a great deal will depend on the type of business, but, in general, the goods will fall into the following categories:

(a) Raw materials (for use in the factory).
(b) Tools.
(c) Machines and other capital items.
(d) Stationery and office equipment.
(e) Consumable stores (such as wrapping paper, oil, string, etc.).
(f) Orders for services such as window cleaning, repair of machines, car hire, advertising, etc.
(g) Where a business is concerned solely with retail trading, the bulk of its purchase will be of manufactured goods for stock.

4. Suppliers. There is seldom any problem in finding a supplier of specific goods, because the trade representatives of manufacturers call on retailers, and buyers (for, say, departmental stores) often tour around the manufacturers to get a better idea of what is on the market.

However, should a retail or wholesale business wish to contact a supplier of goods that have never been purchased before, there are two or three sources:

(*a*) *Trade journals.* Nearly every trade has its own trade journal (such as the *Boot and Shoe Journal*) which carries advertisements by the different manufacturers, as well as carrying articles about new products on the market.

(*b*) *Trade associations.* Mostly, the trade journals are published by the trade association in a particular trade, but if the trade association does not produce a journal it will have a library from which names and addresses of manufacturers can be obtained.

REQUISITION		
Dept....................................		No............................
Please supply the following:		Date..........................
Quantity	Description	Date delivery required
....	....	....
....	....	....
....	....	....
	Authorised signature..	

Fig. 2.— *Requisition note*

(c) *Trade directories.* These are published by the Post Office (one for each area), giving the names and addresses of manufacturers and wholesalers under the trade heading.

5. System in quotation method. When buying is performed by obtaining various quotations from different suppliers, the sequence of events and the documents used will be as follows:

(a) In a large business concern a *requisition* (Fig. 2) will be received by the buying department stating the requirements (it is part of the function of the buying department to collate the requirements of all departments of a business and to buy in bulk).

(b) *Enquiry* letters (*see* Fig. 3) are then sent to selected suppliers (*see* **4** above) asking them to quote price, delivery, etc.

A letter of enquiry should as far as possible:

(i) state definite requirements;

```
                           ENQUIRY                            No.

                     JOHNSON & EDWARDS LTD.
                    High Street, Croydon, Surrey CR9 1BT

    Telephone No. .............   Telegrams .............   Date ........

    To:    The Sales Manager,
           Brown & Co. Ltd.,
           West Street, Bristol BS18 6RG

    Dear Sir,

          This is to ask if you would please quote your best terms for supply of
    the following:
                              C/A Men's Shirts

           1.  Quantity                   2 Doz.      3 Doz.     4 Doz.
           2.  Description of goods   Sizes 15 Blue   16 Green   15 White
           3.  Delivery required       A.S.A.P.
           4.  Terms
           5.  Other notes

                                                  Yours faithfully,

                                                  ..................
                                                  Buying Manager
```

FIG. 3.—*Letter of enquiry.*

(ii) state what the goods are for;
(iii) state terms required (*e.g.* "carriage paid");
(iv) state when delivery is required (if urgent).

III. BUYING

Of course, if recent catalogues of different suppliers are to hand, it may not be necessary to send an enquiry at all, but only an official order.

(c) The suppliers, after receiving the enquiry form, will then send a *quotation*, which will quote the detailed information in answer to the points raised in the enquiry (*see* Fig. 4).

The quotation, when returned, may be accompanied by a sample of the goods the company can supply at the present, which of course may not be the same as those required.

```
                        QUOTATION            No.   2471
                     BROWN & CO. LTD.
                 West Street, Bristol, BS18 6RG.
   Telephone No. ..........  Telegrams ............  Date ..........
```

Catologue No.	Quantity	Description	Delivery (approx.)	Price
1243	2 Doz.	C/A Shirts		
		Blue	14 days	
1436	3 Doz.	" Green		£18 Doz.
1161	4 Doz.	" White		

For acceptance within 14 days
Terms: 2½% 30 days
on approval account
Carriage paid: Croydon

Less 25% Trade Discount

Brown & Co. Ltd.

....
Sales Manager

FIG. 4.—*Quotation.*

(a) "For acceptance within 14 days" is inserted so that the supplier is not bound by his quotation for too long should he wish to increase his price

(b) "Carriage paid: Croydon" means that the supplier pays for the transport of the goods to the station at Croydon, the district in which the buyer has his office. The buyer pays for delivery from the station.

(d) It is an important principle of buying that everything that one wishes to buy must be on an official printed *order* (Fig. 5); this is to prevent unauthorised buying on the company's account.

It will be noticed on the above quotation that the terms include "on approval account"; this means that if the company has not already traded with the particular supplier before, it will be necessary to supply trade references, etc., for the opening of an account (*see* **10** below).

(*e*) Following the placing of the order comes *delivery* of the goods.

(*f*) Either with the goods, or subsequently, an *invoice* will be sent by the suppliers showing the amount of money owing on the order.

```
                          ORDER                    No. 7402

                    JOHNSON & EDWARDS LTD.
                 High Street, Croydon, Surrey, CR9 1BT.
     Telephone No. ..........    Telegrams ............    Date .........

     To:
           The Sales Manager,
           Brown & Co. Ltd.,
           West Street, Bristol BS18 6RG

     Dear Sir,

              Please supply the following:              (Req. No. ....)
```

Quantity	Cat. No.	Description	Price	Delivery
2 Doz.	1243	Men's Shirts C/A Size		
		15 Blue		
3 "	1436	" " "16 Green	£18 Doz.	14 Days
4 "	1161	" " "15 White		

Your Quotation No. 2471......

Terms: 2½% Monthly Account

Delivery: Carriage paid to Croydon

....
Buying Manager

Fig. 5.—*Order*.

(a) All orders are numbered for ease of identification and for quoting on correspondence.
(b) Catalogue numbers, price and delivery must be quoted, as well as terms of payment.
(c) Every order must be signed by the chief buyer, although in many large companies they may be signed by the order clerks on behalf of the company.

6. Sequence of events. Note that the sequence of events when buying on a quotation as set out above is as follows:

(a) Enquiry (for goods required).
(b) Quotation (of price, etc.).
(c) Order (if quotation is satisfactory).
(d) Delivery (of goods).
(e) Invoice (statement of goods supplied and money owing).

7. Tender and contract. Where goods are purchased by tender or on a contract basis, the documents will be similar, except that with the tender method the first step is the placing of *an advertisement* in a newspaper or a trade journal inviting suppliers to tender.

After this, may be sent a *tender form* which has printed headings and terms of the contract.

When a number of tenders have been received by a certain closing date, the one quoting the best prices and terms of delivery is awarded the contract and an official *contract* is then sent to the supplier.

8. A straightforward order. When a regular supplier is known and has been traded with before, or when a sales representative visits the company and has something which the company requires, then an official order may be given straight away without requiring quotation, etc. Often prices, delivery and terms of payment are established beforehand, even over the telephone.

This method is used for small purchases, for anything urgently required, or for special purchases when there may be only one supplier anyway.

9. Terms of payment.
(a) *Trade discount* is the name given to a percentage discount allowed to the buyer off the catalogue price. It is a device to save

the constant reprinting of catalogues, since if it is wished to increase prices all that is necessary is to decrease the trade discount allowed to the buyer. Trade discount is deducted from list price on the invoice. Thus, trade discount represents the profit (or "margin" as it is sometimes called) of the retailer, *i.e.* provided that he sells at the recommended retail price.

(*b*) *Cash discount* is an inducement offered by the supplier to the buyer to pay promptly. Cash discount is not mentioned on the invoice sent to the buyer, and a quotation of $2\frac{1}{2}$-per-cent monthly account means that the buyer can deduct $2\frac{1}{2}$ per cent from the amount stated on the invoice (exclusive of V.A.T.), provided he pays it within one month. This usually means one month from the end of the month in which the goods were received.

10. Buying on credit. It is the custom in business to buy on credit, which means ordering the goods, taking delivery of them, and paying later. Obviously, manufacturers and wholesalers are not going to supply their goods to buyers who cannot pay for them, and so there is a regular procedure for assessing the financial ability of a new customer to settle his account.

When buying on credit from a new supplier, a company must give references to that supplier, in the same way that it would also want similar evidence of ability to pay when *selling* to new customers.

Perhaps the more important aspect of assessing credit is when selling goods to new customers, so the procedure involved is mentioned in Chapter IV in connection with sales.

PROGRESS TEST 3

1. A business buys various categories of goods. Describe these categories. (**3**) [*N.C.T.E.C.*

2. (*a*) State how the buying department of a manufacturing business might obtain the names of suppliers of the commodities it needs.

(*b*) Presuming that for a particular commodity you have found six possible suppliers, draft a letter of enquiry, which can be sent to all six, setting out your requirements. (**4, 5**) [*R.S.A.*

3. What are the relationships between a quotation and an order? (**5**) [*N.C.T.E.C.*

4. (*a*) List the information that should be supplied by a letter requesting a quotation for goods.

(b) Why should a firm set at the foot of its quotation the words "For acceptance within fourteen days"? (**5**) [*U.E.I.*

5. The purchasing officer of your firm is asked to order a specific quantity of a new material. What documents and procedures will be involved up to the time the goods are paid for? (**5, 6**) [*E.M.E.U.*

6. The steps followed when a firm buys goods are *order, quotation, payment, enquiry, delivery*. Rewrite these steps in the correct chronological order, explaining the purpose of each. (**5, 6**) [*U.E.I.*

7. A buyer is offered goods by one supplier at 15-per-cent trade discount, ready delivery, cash one month net, carriage paid. Another supplier offers goods at the same price with 25-per-cent trade discount, two months' delivery, carriage forward and 5-per-cent cash discount within ten days from date of invoice. What factors will the buyer have to take into account in deciding which of the quotations to accept? In your answer show that you understand the terms used above. (**9**)

[*R.S.A.*

8. A company finds it necessary to buy an item of equipment costing £20,000. If it buys for cash it will receive a 5-per-cent cash discount but will leave itself rather short of ready money. The company has also made enquiries about hire purchase terms and credit sale agreements but has not yet decided what to do. Set out the arguments for and against the three methods of payment indicated above. Show clearly that you know the meaning of the terms used. (**9**) [*R.S.A.*

(Hire purchase and credit sales are dealt with in the next chapter.)

CHAPTER IV
SALES

1. Sales and marketing. Sometimes the sales department is known as the "marketing department", and, while the sales function has already been mentioned in Chapter II, marketing is the wider term and, as well as the control of sales, includes:

(*a*) advertising;
(*b*) warehousing;
(*c*) transport;
(*d*) packaging;
(*e*) market research.

In large business concerns, there may be separate departments with each of these titles, in addition to a sales department.

2. Sales department. To reiterate, the function of the sales department is as follows:

(*a*) To ascertain what customers want to buy (assessing the market).

(*b*) To see if such products can be obtained (or made).

(*c*) To let possible purchasers know of the company's products.

(*d*) To persuade them to buy the products (*see* **4** and **5** below).

(*e*) To see that the goods are delivered to them in accordance with orders received.

3. Organisation of a sales department. There can be no standard organisation of a sales department because it will depend on the size of the company, on its products and on the policy of top management. But a typical organisation might well be as follows:

(*a*) Order section (where orders are received from customers—increasingly over the telephone).

(*b*) Invoice checking section.

(*c*) Advertising section.

(d) Catalogue and filing section.
(e) General clerical and typing section.
(f) Credit control section (*see* **6** below).
(g) The sales manager. He will be greatly involved in supervision and control of the sales representatives, who report to him perhaps once a week.

4. Advertising. The sales department is usually in charge of the advertising department (sometimes called the "publicity department"), which is concerned with methods of attracting customers.

Many kinds of advertising are used, according to the finances of the company, its type of product and the size of the market sought after, but the most usual are the following:

(a) Television advertising. This is the most effective method, and the most expensive.

(b) Press and poster advertising. Advertisements must be inserted in the most appropriate publications, whether these are national and local newspapers, trade journals, or general interest magazines. This method is cheaper than television advertising.

(c) Cinema and radio advertising. Cinema advertising is particularly useful for local businesses. Radio advertising is used by both local and national business interests.

5. Public relations department. This department also takes part in advertising, but its scope is much wider, for it deals with such things as the following:

(a) Press conferences and sending editorial matter to the press.

(b) Recruitment brochures and company newspapers or journals (house magazines).

(c) Sending speakers to conferences, schools, etc.

(d) Ensuring a good after-sales service and dealing with complaints from customers.

(e) Publicity campaigns, such as the sponsoring of sporting events in horse racing, golf, motor racing, etc.

(f) Taking part in trade exhibitions.

The whole purpose of the public relations department is to build up and maintain the goodwill of the public and of customers towards the company and its products.

6. Credit control. Most businesses these days have a credit control section of the sales department, and in fact many have a separate official known as the "credit controller".

The function of credit control is as follows:

(*a*) To assess the creditworthiness of new customers (*i.e.* whether it is advisable to let them have goods on credit and to what amount of money).

(*b*) To exercise continuous control over credit already allowed to customers (*i.e.* to see if they are settling their debts promptly).

The whole purpose of credit control is to prevent the creation of *bad debts*, *i.e.* sums of money owing to company which will not be received because the debtor is unable to pay for the goods supplied to him.

7. Methods of credit control. When a new customer places an order for the first time and wishes to buy goods on credit, the credit controller will use two or more of the following:

(*a*) *Trader's reference.* The new customer is asked for the name and address of another trader who can be written to and asked for his assessment of the customer for the granting of credit.

(*b*) *Bank reference.* The new customer is asked for the name and address of his bank, so that an enquiry can be made (through one's own bank) as to the customer's financial standing. A direct application to a customer's bank would not be answered, since it might be indiscreet for them to give information on a customer to an outsider, but it would be given if requested by another bank (*i.e.* one's own bank).

(*c*) *Status enquiry agents.* These are well-known business firms (such as Stubbs' and Bradstreet's) who for a fee will give a report on the financial standing and history of the new customer.

(*d*) *Trade associations.* Some of these will give information about customers, and in fact some maintain a "blacklist" of customers who are known to have defaulted in payment of debts to other traders.

When the replies to these enquiries are received, the credit controller will assess the possibility of payment compared with the cost of the goods ordered, and will approve credit up to (say) £50 only, and an entry may be made to that effect on the customer's order record.

However, once a customer has been supplied with goods, perhaps repeatedly over a long period, it is still necessary to check on whether he is settling his account promptly, *i.e.* whether he is able to pay for the goods supplied. To this end, a list of debtors at the end of each month is usually obtained from the accounts department. This list is usually analysed by the date and amount of each debt. While a total of £100 outstanding with £95 last month and £5 from three months ago is not so worrying, if it is with £95 from three months ago and £5 last month then some immediate action has to be taken to obtain payment of the outstanding amount.

Usually, the action taken takes the form of a series of standard *credit letters*, perhaps numbered, 1, 2 and 3, which are sent out at regular intervals after the debt is overdue, and the third letter of which threatens legal proceedings if the debt is not paid.

8. Extended credit. Some companies selling such things as washing machines and television sets offer what is known as "extended credit terms". This means that instead of the normal one-month credit allowed in the trade they offer the customer perhaps nine months to pay for the goods purchased.

This policy is followed mainly to avoid government restrictions which would apply if the goods were sold on hire purchase (*see* **9** below), but also to attract customers by the relatively low price.

With extended credit, ownership in the goods passes to the customers immediately they take delivery of them, and if the customer defaults in his monthly payments the only recourse of the business is to sue the customer for non-payment in a court of law.

NOTE: Ordinary credit sales allow customers only a short term of credit, perhaps a month or even seven or ten days.

9. Hire purchase. Many people find it difficult to save or find the purchase price of expensive goods, and so hire purchase was introduced to allow a customer to make a deposit or downpayment and then sign a hire purchase agreement by which he agrees to make weekly or monthly payments for so many months or years.

It is called "hire purchase" because the ownership of the goods belongs to the selling company (or very often with an intermediary hire purchase finance company) and the goods are only on hire to the customer while he is making payments. Ownership in the goods does not pass to the customer until the very last payment has been made (note the difference between ownership and possession).

If the customer defaults in his repayments, the company can take back the goods since they belong to them and have not been paid for. However, to prevent unscrupulous traders from taking the goods back when nearly paid for, and perhaps selling them to another customer, the *Hire Purchase Act* 1938 laid down that:

(*a*) a customer can return the goods to the seller provided he has paid at least half the purchase price;

(*b*) if more than one-third of the total amount has been paid, and the customer finds that he cannot maintain the payments, then the article can be reclaimed by the seller only if a court order is obtained (the court usually makes an order for repayment of smaller amounts of money).

Further legislation has decreed that:

(*a*) the cash price for all goods has to be clearly shown to the customer, so that he can see how much extra he is paying for the hire purchase facility; and

(*b*) three days are allowed (in certain circumstances) from the signing of a hire purchase agreement in which it can be rescinded (this is to prevent unscrupulous door-step salesmen from forcing hire purchase sales on gullible housewives).

10. Advantages and disadvantages of hire purchase.

(*a*) *Advantages:*

(*i*) Although buying on hire purchase is quite an expensive way of obtaining goods, it has the advantage to the customer that the goods must be maintained by the selling company while repayments are being made (the goods belong to the seller). This is particularly useful with mechanical things such as record-players and cars.

(*ii*) To the business concern, it represents a means of selling expensive goods which otherwise might not be sold at all.

(*b*) *Disadvantages:*

(*i*) The customer is often charged an exorbitant rate of interest when it is calculated on the full cash price (as it always is) and not on the reducing balance of the amount owing as repayments are made.

(*ii*) To the trader, it represents a loss of working capital, since it may be a year or so before he receives payment for goods sold (although most businesses today make use of hire purchase finance companies which advance the money to the trader for replenishing his stock and which take over the hire purchase debt from the customer).

(*iii*) It may encourage customers to buy more goods than they can really afford.

11. Sales procedure.

(*a*) A customer can place an *order* for goods either with the company's sales representative on his travels, through the post, or, increasingly today, over the telephone; or the order may be as the result of a quotation previously supplied.

(*b*) On receipt of the customer's order, it is usual to send an *acknowledgment of order* setting out details of goods ordered and quoting delivery and terms of payment.

(*c*) If the customer is a new one, the *credit control* section will assess the customer's credit standing and will approve or disallow the order (the company want to sell goods, but not at the risk of bad debts).

(*d*) If credit is approved, a copy of the customer's order is sent to the factory, showroom or warehouse for despatch, giving instructions about delivery method, time and address, etc. It is often necessary for the customer's order to be "interpreted" in terms of the company's catalogue number and specification, etc. (customers do not always quote the catalogue number or use proper descriptions).

(*e*) When the goods are ready for delivery, they are accompanied by a *delivery note* (Fig. 6), so that the customer can check the goods actually received with what the company sent (sometimes some goods get lost *en route*). As well as a delivery note, some companies use a form which is an exact copy of it but which is called a *receipt note*. The customer is required to sign this, after which it is then returned to the sales department as evidence that goods have been delivered.

```
                    DELIVERY NOTE            No.

                       BROWN & CO. LTD.
                   West Street, Bristol, BS18 6RG.

                                          Date ...................

To:   Johnson & Edwards Ltd.,
      12 High Street,
      Croydon, Surrey CR9 1BT


Please receive:                         (Your Order No. 7402.)
```

Cat. No.	Quantity	Description	
1243	2 Doz.	Men's Shirts C/A Size 15 Blue	
1436	3 Doz.	" " " " 16 Green	To follow
1161	4 Doz.	" " " " 15 White	

```
                                   Delivery:  Own Van
```

FIG. 6.—*Delivery note.*

The goods listed are usually a copy of the full order, but if some goods are not in stock they may be marked (as above) "To follow."

(*f*) An *advice note* is a carbon copy of a delivery note except for its heading. When goods are sent by rail or by road transport, an advice note is sent by post to the customer so that he will have this before the goods are received, and will know that the goods are on the way. This saves the customer telephoning and enquiring when his goods are likely to be received.

(*g*) Either with the goods or subsequently, an *invoice* is sent to the customer for the goods supplied (*see* Fig. 7).

NOTE: One of the principles of office systems is to reduce the amount of office work as much as possible, and so many business concerns do not make up a delivery note, advice note, invoice, etc., separately. This would take too long and waste time, and so by using carbon paper and perhaps continuous stationery it is usual to type simultaneously:

  (*i*) invoice;
  (*ii*) delivery note;
  (*iii*) copy for accounts department (for the purpose of posting to the Sales Ledger which contains records of what is owing from a customer).

IV. SALES

```
                    INVOICE              No. 1241.

              BROWN & CO. LTD.
            West Street, Bristol, BS18 6RG.

Telephone No. ............ Telegrams ............ Date ..........

To:  Johnson & Edwards Ltd.,
     12 High Street,
     Croydon, Surrey CR9 1BT

                                          (Your Order No. 7402)
```

Cat. No.	Quantity	Description	Price	Trade discount	Amount
					£
1243	2 Doz.	Men's Shirts C/A Size 15 Blue	£18	25%	27.00
1436	3 "	Men's Shirts C/A Size 16 Green	£18	"	40.50
1161	4 "	Men's Shirts C/A Size 15 White	£18	"	54.00
					121.50

```
                              V.A.T. 8% on gross    9.72
                                                  ──────
                                                   131.22
                                     Packing        0.50
                                                  ──────
                                                  £131.72
                                                  ══════

Delivery:   Own van - 29th June  197-
            Carriage paid
Terms:      2½% Monthly Account
            E. and O.E.
```

FIG. 7.—*Invoice.*

(*a*) It is important to quote the customer's order number because this enables him to identify the order.

(*b*) Trade discount is featured on the invoice, but *not* cash discount, which is deductible by the purchaser only if paid within the terms of account (*i.e.* one month in the above example).

(*c*) "E. and O.E." stands for *errors and omissions excepted* and means that the invoice is correct apart from any errors or omissions committed. It has no legal significance and any mistakes must be rectified (*see* Chapter VIII).

In addition, other copies may also be typed at the same time for:

(*iv*) advice note;

(*v*) copy for the transport department (who have to arrange deliveries);

(*vi*) copy for factory or warehouse (to make up goods);

(*vii*) copy for the sales representative, to keep him informed of what a customer in his area has ordered.

(*h*) When goods are returned as unsuitable or where chargeable empties are returned by customers, then a *credit note* is issued (usually printed in red) which gives the customer an allowance for the value stated on it. In the company's books of account a credit note is the opposite of an invoice, for where the former gives an allowance of money the latter makes a charge.

(*i*) The invoice is not usually a request for payment but more of a statement of what is owing. When a customer agrees to pay cash instead of buying on credit, then a *pro forma invoice* is sent, which does then amount to a request for payment.

```
                        STATEMENT

                      BROWN & CO. LTD.
                  West Street, Bristol, BS18 6RG.

  To:    Johnson & Edwards Ltd.,
         12 High Street,
         Croydon, Surrey CR9 1BT

                                               Dr.      Cr.
```

Date	Balance b/f		224.50	
197–				
June 9	Invoice No. 1205		23.25	
" 15	" " " 1241		131.72	
" 26	" " " 1317		50.50	
			229.97	
June 7	Cash and Discount			24.50
		BALANCE DUE	205.47	

FIG. 8.—*Statement*.

(*a*) The statement is really a copy of what the seller posts in his Sales Ledger, *i.e.* all goods sold on credit at different times in the month, as well as cash received.

(*b*) It brings forward any amount owing at the beginning of the month and deducts any cash received since then.

(*c*) No details of goods supplied are entered on the statement, only references to the different invoices representing different sales.

After the invoice, and usually at the end of the month in which the sales were made, a monthly *statement* of account is sent which summarises all the invoices and trading carried on during the month (*see* Fig. 8). This *is* a request for payment, and cash discount is usually deducted by the buyer from this statement.

(*j*) Upon receipt of the statement, or very shortly afterwards, the customer should send his cheque in payment of the balance owing, usually returning the statement at the same time. If invoices cannot be agreed, however, they will be deducted from the statement, and only the cleared invoices will be paid for.

12. V.A.T. (Value Added Tax). Manufacturers, wholesalers and importers dealing in goods which are subject to V.A.T. must register with the Inland Revenue Department of the Government. The amount of tax is the current rate (at present 8%) on the value "added" by the business, *i.e.* the difference between the buying and selling price. Thus, if a timber merchant sells timber to a furniture manufacturer for £100, he must add 8% to his invoice, making it £108. Then, if the furniture manufacturer sells his furniture to a retailer for, say, £250, he must add 8%, making it £270. The manufacturer will have to pay the difference between the V.A.T. which he has paid (£8) and the £20 which he is charging his customers, a difference of £12.

If a business has a turnover of less than £5,000, it need not register for paying V.A.T., although it will still be charged V.A.T. on its purchases. Some goods and services are exempt, *i.e.* the seller is not registered, does not charge V.A.T. on his sales and cannot reclaim V.A.T. paid on purchases; while some other classes of business are "zero-rated"; these are registered and again do not charge V.A.T. on sales, but can reclaim tax paid on purchases.

13. Common abbreviations.

(*a*) *c.o.d.* This stands for "cash on delivery", and when it is quoted it means that it is a cash sale, cash being payable when the goods are delivered. The Post Office provides a special *c.o.d.* service by which they will collect cash on behalf of the seller.

(*b*) *c.w.o.* This stands for "cash with order" and means that the order must be prepaid, or in other words that the cash payable must be sent with the order, credit not being allowed.

14. Export sales. Where goods are exported under a "documentary credit" arrangement, the usual practice is for the exporter to inform the foreign importer that he has opened a bank credit in his favour at a specified bank in the importer's country. The importer can then obtain payment by "drawing" on this credit, provided the following documents are sent him to present to the named bank:

(a) A set of "clean bills of lading", which evidences shipment ("clean" means that the goods are undamaged).

(b) A commercial invoice.

(c) An insurance policy covering marine risks.

(d) A consular invoice (required by some countries only) which is certified by a consul of the importer's country with an office in the exporter's country and which certifies that the goods are in order for export to his country.

(e) Perhaps a certificate of origin certifying the country of manufacture, etc.

(f) A bill of exchange.

These documents are sent to the exporter, after the goods have been despatched, which will then enable the foreign exporter to obtain immediate payment at the bank specified.

PROGRESS TEST 4

1. (a) State how the sales department of a business might attract customers.
(b) What essential information would the sales department need to include in its quotation or estimates? (**4**) [*R.S.A.*

2. What precautions should be taken before granting credit to customers? (**6**) [*U.L.C.I.*

3. (a) Why is it important to keep overdue accounts to a minimum?
(b) What steps should be taken when accounts are outstanding for a long period? (**6**) [*Y.C.F.E.*

4. You have received an order for £200 worth of goods from V. Doubtful Ltd. You have not done business with this company before and know nothing of its financial circumstances. What action do you recommend before executing this order? (**6**) [*Y.C.F.E.*

5. Outline the differences between purchase and credit sales. (**8, 9**)
 [*U.L.C.I.*

6. Write brief notes on (a) credit sales, (b) extended credit sales and (c) hire purchase. (**8, 9**) [*N.C.T.E.C.*

7. Explain the hire purchase method of selling. What are its advantages and disadvantages? (**9, 10**) [*Y.C.F.E.*

8. A new member of your typing staff has just typed six invoices in triplicate. She asks you the following questions:
(a) What is an invoice? What is it for?
(b) Why did I have to type them in triplicate?
Answer her as clearly as you can. (**11**) [*R.S.A.*

9. Explain briefly the meaning of the following terms: (a) display allowance, (b) V.A.T., (c) cash discount, (d) advice note (e) c.w.o. (**11, 12, 13**) [*R.S.A.*

10. Explain the terms: (a) letter of enquiry, (b) acknowledgment, (c) credit note, (d) statement. (**11**) [*U.L.C.I.*

11. (a) What is the essential difference between a sale for cash and a sale on credit?

(b) Mention, and briefly describe, the documents which would pass between the buyer and the seller from the beginning to the end of a monthly credit transaction. (**11**) [*Y.C.F.E.*

12. Explain the following terms: *pro-forma* invoice, credit note. (**11**) [*Y.C.F.E.*

13. Prepare an invoice with appropriate details relating to the sale of the following items:

    4 Axminster carpets 4 yd × 3 yd @ £124 ea.
    6 Wilton carpets 3 yd × 3 yd @ £127 ea.
    12 hearth rugs 54 in. × 27 in. @£16 ea.

The invoice is to be subject to 25-per-cent trade discount and $2\frac{1}{2}$-per cent cash discount if paid within one month from the date of the invoice. Delivery will be by passenger train—carriage paid. (**11**)
[*E.M.E.U.*

14. What courses of action are open to a sales clerk when he receives an order from a customer who has no credit account but has not sent cash with his order? (**10, 6**) [*N.C.T.E.C.*

15. Outline the work involved from the receipt of an enquiry for goods until the order has been carried out. (**11**) [*N.C.T.E.C.*

16. What is the relationship between an invoice and a statement? (**11**) [*N.C.T.E.C.*

17. The following errors are made by a supplier in sending goods to his customers. Describe in detail how the errors would be rectified and the documents which would be used:

    (a) The supplier invoices ten cases but sent only nine.

    (b) One case contains 100 articles at £0·25 each instead of £0·30.

    (c) One invoice is overcast to the extent of £10.

    (d) Trade discount of 10 per cent is omitted on one invoice but the customer has deducted this on paying it. (**11**) [*U.E.I.*

18. Describe the following: c.w.o., c.o.d., f.o.r., ex works, c.i.f. (**13**)
[*U.L.C.I.*

19. Your firm has recently shipped 1,000 bags of flour to a Mr Smith c.i.f. Lagos, the terms being that Mr Smith will remit "cash against documents". List the documents which you would forward to Mr Smith in order to obtain payment, giving a brief description and stating the purpose of each. (**14**) [*U.E.I.*

CHAPTER V

TRANSPORT

1. Transport and its importance. Transport is an important aspect of commerce without which all other aspects would be greatly handicapped.

Away from coastal areas, the railways first opened up the hinterland of vast continents. With the advent of road transport carriage of goods has been made easier and more convenient still, and with the growth of air transport it has become faster than ever, and no place need be out of reach of urban areas any longer.

Modern business has the choice of road, rail, sea (river) and air transport, each of which has its own advantages and disadvantages. It is important to know which kind of transport is most suitable for particular goods being sent to a particular destination.

Improved transport has affected the *location of industry*, although it is no longer necessary for a factory to be built close to a river (although useful for effluent) or railway as in the eighteenth and nineteenth centuries.

Good transport makes easier the *supply of raw materials* to factories, as well as the distribution of their *manufactured goods*.

Transport *for the workers* has also had an influence on the location of industries as well as the siting of new towns.

Transport can be classified into three categories:

(*a*) *Home* transport (inside the country) using road, rail, air, canals, rivers and sea.

(*b*) *Overseas* transport, using the sea and air (and incidentally road and rail to and from the ship).

(*c*) *Postal* services; many businesses send their goods, if in small parcels, both home and overseas by ordinary postal services.

2. Road transport. There are two main methods of transporting goods by road:

(*a*) By a private or public road haulage company (often called a "common carrier"); British Road Services is the largest road haulage company in Britain, and there are specialised road services for different kinds of goods: B.R.S. (Parcels) Ltd. for small parcels, B.R.S. (Meat Haulage) Ltd. for meat, and B.R.S. (Pickfords) Ltd. for heavy loads.

(*b*) By a company using its own vans.

3. Transport Act 1968. This Act introduced a National Freight Corporation to integrate the nationalised road and rail services. Besides offering the customer co-ordinated road and rail services, it aimed at eliminating duplication between these services.

(*a*) *Quantity licensing.* If lorries of over 16 tons go on journeys over the statutory 100-mile limit, then special authorisation must be obtained from a licensing board. The obvious aim of this provision is to force heavy loads to be transported by rail rather than by road.

(*b*) *Road transport licensing.* Small lorries under 30 cwt no longer need to obtain a special carrier's licence (*see* **4** below). But lorries of over 30 cwt are subject to quantity licensing, and the granting of a licence depends on the owner's fitness to keep his lorries in safe condition, and not to break the rules about driving hours.

(*c*) *Driver's hours.* Maximum hours for lorry drivers are 11 hours daily (10 hours actual driving). This is based on road safety and to prevent lorries being driven long distances by over-tired drivers.

4. Road transport authorities. The National Freight Corporation is responsible for fifty-three transport companies including Freightliner, National Carriers and British Road Services. It is the largest organisation in the field, but does not have a monopoly, for it must compete commercially with the rest of the private road transport industry.

There are two major parcel carrying services:

(*a*) National Carriers Limited, which uses rail transport for about 85% of its long-distance business, and

(*b*) British Road Services Parcels, which is essentially a road-based long-distance carrier.

In a Government report on these services, there has been some criticism of the overlapping of their facilities.

Currently, there is still controversy over the size of the so-called "juggernaut" articulated lorries (as used on the Continent). While economical to run, they are said to be a danger on the road and destructive to the environment because of their noise, vibration etc.

5. Company road transport. Only big business concerns will have their own fleets of lorries, and usually there will be a transport department with a transport manager. Control over such transport will be necessary to ensure that no goods are taken away without proper authorisation, that best use is made of the vehicles, that the vehicles are kept in good running order and that deliveries are made systematically according to a daily or weekly programme.

A system for the control of a company's own transport will include the following:

(*a*) Records of each vehicle, together with its running costs, *i.e.* petrol and oil (use of a special log book).

(*b*) Maintenance records of each vehicle, to ensure regular and systematic servicing.

(*c*) Mileage records of each vehicle, so that cost per mile can be calculated (daily journey sheets).

(*d*) Weighbridge tickets.

(*e*) The issue of despatch copy of the invoices which authorise the taking of goods.

(*f*) Records of goods delivered and goods returned (there is often a receipt note signed by the customer as proof of delivery).

It is common practice to have a weighbridge at the entrance to a factory (particularly where heavy and bulky goods are transported) and to ensure that every lorry going out stops to have its weight checked. By deducting the unladen weight of the lorry from the weight recorded on the *weighbridge ticket*, it is then possible to calculate the net weight of the goods taken out. The weighbridge tickets for one day are usually collected the following morning, and the weights indicated are used for invoicing purposes.

When a company has its own petrol station, then a simple log book will be needed to record the quantities of petrol and oil supplied to each vehicle (*see* Fig. 9). As an alternative, some companies have an account with a local garage where the vans collect petrol and oil and charge it to the company account.

LOG BOOK OF PETROL AND OIL								
Date	Reg. No. of van	Gals. petrol	Price	Total	Pints oil	Price	Total	Driver's signature

Fig. 9.—*Log book of petrol and oil.*

6. Efficiency of own transport. From the above information, it should be apparent that in checking on the efficiency of its own transport, a company will need to know the daily costs per vehicle of its consumption of petrol and oil, as well as costs of maintenance and repair.

All this must then be compared with the mileage covered by each vehicle. This is usually entered by the driver on his *daily journey sheet*, so that it is a simple calculation to discover the cost per mile of running each vehicle.

However, efficiency may also be assessed by the number of complaints received about slow deliveries or non-deliveries.

7. Advantages of road transport.

(*a*) It is generally cheaper than rail transport (especially for expensive and bulky goods).

(*b*) Road haulage provides a door-to-door service, which eliminates subsequent loading and unloading (as may be necessary with rail transport).

(*c*) The goods do not need to be so carefully packed as when being sent by rail.

(*d*) Usually it is also the quickest means of transport (this applies more to short distances than to those of 100 miles or more).

(e) Special lorries suited to the goods conveyed can be used, *e.g.* petrol tankers, milk tankers.

8. Disadvantages of road transport.

(a) From a national point of view, it means congestion on the roads.

(b) There are many difficulties accompanying the running of one's own transport, such as maintenance of vehicles, making full use of them, and depreciation.

(c) For very bulky goods (portable buildings, etc.) it may be dangerous (low bridges, narrow winding roads, etc.).

(d) It is not the quickest for long journeys (*e.g.* rail transport can take goods from London to Newcastle in five hours).

9. Rail transport. Goods for transport by rail may be despatched by:

(a) goods train—usually for heavy, bulky goods; or

(b) passenger train—usually for smaller, lighter parcels, which are carried in the guard's van; this method, however, is dearer than sending by goods train, although it is quicker.

When it is wished to send goods by rail, all that it is necessary to do is to telephone the parcels office of the nearest railway station, and they will send a British Rail van to collect. However, if delivery of goods is urgent, it is better to take them to the station for despatch.

When sending goods by rail, evidence of their receipt at the sending station is given by British Rail on a *consignment note* which bears the sender's name and address; the name and address to which the goods are being sent, the number and description of packages, the destination station and the weight (which determine the charge, as well as the distance).

10. Rail charges. Railway charges for transport depend on the following factors:

(a) Method used (*e.g.* passenger or goods train).

(b) Type of goods (different classes of goods have different rates).

(c) Weight of goods.

(d) Distance conveyed.

(e) Degree of risk (*see* below).

Railways' charges were once (in the public interest) narrowly prescribed by law, but since the *Transport Act* of 1962 greater freedom has been given to the railways to charge whatever rates they agree with their customers.

The seller of goods (*i.e.* the sender) will always pay for the rail transport, but whether he actually bears the cost or charges it to his customer depends on what is stated on the quotation to the customer. Thus:

(*a*) *"carriage paid"* means that the seller will bear the cost of transport. Sometimes, it is, for example, "Carriage paid Manchester Central Station" when the seller pays cost of transport to the buyer's nearest station, but the buyer must bear the cost of local delivery from the station;

(*b*) *"carriage forward"* means that the seller will pay for the cost of transport, but will include such cost on the invoice of the goods delivered so that the charge is borne by the customer.

11. Company's risk and owner's risk. When sending goods by rail, the sender can choose between two different rates of charge:

(*a*) *Company's risk* (C.R.), where the railway is responsible for the safe delivery of the goods and of course must compensate the sender if the goods are damaged or lost *en route*.

(*b*) *Owner's risk* (O.R.), where the railway is responsible only for damage or loss of goods due to the deliberate negligence or dishonesty of its employees. For compensation under O.R., it is necessary to prove the negligence or dishonesty of the railway employees—a very difficult thing to do.

Of course, the rates charged for (*b*) are lower than those for (*a*).

12. Advantages of rail transport.

(*a*) Although generally more expensive than sending goods by road, rail transport may be *cheaper* for heavy bulky goods over long distances.

(*b*) Again, for long distances, rail transport is much *quicker*.

(*c*) The railways have their own "container" transport (whereby goods are loaded into big transport cases at the sender's door and not unloaded until they reach the customer) and special container transport for such things as milk, oil and cement. Where factories are close to a railway, and have their own sidings, it is obviously convenient to send heavy, bulky raw material by rail.

13. Disadvantages of rail transport.

(a) It is generally *expensive* to send goods over short distances by rail.

(b) Goods may have to be taken to the railway station, or await collection by the railway van, which means *delay*.

(c) The loading and unloading at each end of the railway transport gives opportunity for damage or loss of goods.

(d) If the customer (or the seller) is some distance from a railway station, it may present difficulty or at any rate cause delay in delivery from the railway station.

14. Sea, river and canal transport. Carriage by water, whether it be by river, canal or by sea, is cheaper than by other means, but it is interesting to note that when canals were built they actually provided a quicker means of transport than by road.

When railways were constructed, many of the canals were abandoned, and although there are some notable ones still widely used (such as the Manchester Ship Canal) they are generally too slow for modern purposes.

However, when a company is regularly consigning heavy bulky goods such as timber, gravel and coal, water transport is still used and the following methods are available:

(a) *Coastal steamers* which trade between different ports of the U.K.

(b) *Ocean-going liners* which ply between ports in the U.K. and countries all over the world.

(c) *Tramp steamers* which have regular schedules on regular routes between different countries, and which are open to carry any goods requested anywhere.

(d) *Company ships* owned particularly by large companies importing such things as oil and who use huge specially built oil tankers.

V. TRANSPORT

15. Shipping documents. First of all, goods will have to be sent to a port, either by road or by rail, when a *consignment note* will be needed (*see* **5**, above). If sent by rail, an *advice note* will be sent by the railway authority to the company stating that the goods have been received at the docks.

As soon as the advice note is received, the consigners will send a *shipping note* to the docks (*see* Fig. 10).

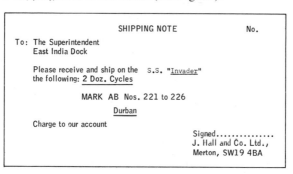

FIG. 10.—*Shipping note.*

The company will in arrangement with a shipping company make out a *bill of lading*, which is a receipt for the goods but which in addition is used as a document of title; *i.e.* the person in possession of the bill of lading is the person entitled to the goods, and property in the goods may be transferred by endorsement and delivery of the bill.

When the bill of lading is presented to the shipping company, they will issue a *freight note*, which notifies the charges payable (*see* Fig. 11).

16. Advantages of water transport.

(*a*) It offers a *cheap* form of transport, particularly for heavy bulky goods such as clay, sand and gravel.

(*b*) It is a *smooth* and fairly *safe* method of transport.

(*c*) It is the *only means* of *overseas* transport (apart, of course, from air).

(*d*) When a factory (saw-mill, etc.) is on the river's edge (as it often is), it may be the most convenient method.

```
                        FREIGHT NOTE           No.
                                        Date ..............
J. Hall & Co. Ltd.,
Merton, SW19 4BA

Dr. to John T. Davey & Co. Ltd.,
       Agent for the Caledonian Line of Steamers

Freight per  S.S. "Invader"
```

Marks and Nos.	Packages	Description	cu m	Rate	Amount
AB Durban Nos. 221-226	6	Cases Cycles PRIMAGE 10%	10	£18	£180.00 18.00 £198.00

FIG. 11.—*Freight note*.
(*a*) 11 cu. m. at 1·1 cu. m. to 1000 kg. equals 10,000 kg. at £18 per 1000.
(Different commodities have different conversion weights.)
(*b*) Primage is a charge made for handling, loading, etc.

17. Disadvantages of water transport.

(*a*) It is *slow*, not so much because of the speed of the ship, barge, etc., but because of the delays in loading and unloading.

(*b*) It may *not always* be *convenient*, *e.g.* if a factory is inland and away from the sea, river or canal.

(*c*) It may *not always* be *suitable*, *e.g.* for very small or valuable goods.

(*d*) It is more subject to the *vagaries of the weather*, *e.g.* ice, fog.

(*e*) *More clerical work* is required; *i.e.* more form-filling is usual when sending goods by sea than by other means.

18. Air transport. An increasing amount of goods is now being consigned by air, both inside Britain and abroad. A company can transport its goods by various means:

(*a*) British Airways, a public corporation which has regular services (*i.e.* scheduled flights) to countries all over the world.

(*b*) Non-scheduled or "charter flights" by private airlines carry goods for other people as and when required.

(c) Some companies even have their own aeroplane transport.

19. Advantages of air transport.

(a) It is the *fastest* method of transport (although if the airport is some distance from the customer the time taken in transporting *from* the airport often exceeds the flight time). It is particularly useful for sending such things as spare parts for machines urgently required.

(b) It is particularly useful for sending *perishable* goods such as flowers.

(c) *Smoothness* of transport means that it is very suitable for sending eggs, livestock, etc.

(d) It has the advantage of *security*: opportunities for pilfering are less than when goods are sent either by road or by rail.

20. Disadvantages of air transport.

(a) *Cost*. The cost of air transport is still relatively high, and makes air transport generally more suitable for small valuable goods such as jewellery, drugs, etc.

(b) *Limitation of capacity*. Although aeroplanes tend to become ever larger in size, they still cannot compete with the capacity of ships or barges.

(c) *Risk*. There is probably a high degree of risk, and insurance will cost more than when sending by rail or by sea.

(d) *Unreliability*. Air transport is not always reliable, because it is subject even more than water transport to climatic conditions.

21. Methods of quotation. When quoting prices on a tender, it is very important that the degree to which the consignor will pay for transport should be indicated. Thus, what seems to be a low price when quoted "ex works" may in fact be dear when compared with a "carriage paid" or c.i.f. quotation. The various methods of quotation are as follows:

(a) *Ex works* (sometimes called "loco") means the basic price of the goods at the factory exclusive of any transport charges afterwards.

(b) f.o.r. stands for "free on rail", which means that the seller will pay for transporting the goods from his factory to the railway station, and that the buyer must then pay for rail charges and delivery at his end from the station.

(c) *f.a.s.* stands for "free alongside ship", which means that the price includes transport to the docks (by road or rail), but exclusive of loading charges or freight.

(d) *f.o.b.* stands for "free on board", which is the same as f.a.s., except that it includes the cost of loading on the ship.

(e) *c. and f.* stands for "cost and freight", which is the same as f.o.b., but it also includes the cost of sending goods by sea (freight).

(f) *c.i.f.* stands for "cost, insurance and freight", which price includes marine insurance and freight, leaving the foreign buyer to pay for unloading and collection from the docks in his country.

(g) *Franco* means "free", indicating that the quotation includes all transport charges to the customer in the importer's country and is free of any other transport charge to the importer.

PROGRESS TEST 5

1. Discuss the various methods of transport available to a businessman when delivering goods to his home and export customers. (**2, 9, 14, 18**) [*U.E.I.*

2. In connection with transport records, what are: (*a*) driver's log sheets, weighbridge tickets, (*b*) daily journey sheets? (**2–5**)
[*N.C.T.E.C.*

3. Draw up a simple log to record the quantities of petrol and diesel oil supplied daily to a firm's own vehicles.
Make *five* specimen entries, including commercial vehicles and travellers' cars. (**5**) [*N.C.T.E.C.*

4. You work in the despatch department of a large manufacturing company. Describe the office routine involved in the despatch, by various means, of goods for the home market. (**5, 9**) [*E.M.E.U.*

5. The methods of inland transport are: road, rail, canal and air. These methods are not equally suitable for all kinds of goods. Mention a few of the advantages and disadvantages of each method, giving an example of goods that could suitably be carried in each case. (**7, 8, 12, 13, 16, 17**) [*U.E.I.*

6. A small but growing retail business is considering the purchase of a delivery van to make daily deliveries to customers within a ten-mile radius. What documents will be needed and what sort of system must be adopted to see that this part of the business is efficiently conducted and that customers are satisfied? (**5**) [*R.S.A.*

7. Explain the terms: (*a*) owner's risk, (*b*) carriage forward, (*c*) proof of delivery, (*d*) consignment note. (**9–11**) [*U.L.C.I.*

8. Name *four* documents which may be used in the carriage of goods and give a short description of the use of each. (**15**) [*U.L.C.I.*

9. What are the differences in buying goods carriage paid as compared with carriage forward?
What is the difference between owner's and company's risk? (**10, 11**)
[*N.C.T.E.C.*

10. Explain the meaning of the terms: (*a*) f.o.b., (*b*) owner's risk, (*c*) forward delivery, (*d*) carriage forward, (*e*) bill of lading. (**10, 11, 15, 21**)
[*R.S.A.*

11. In connection with the carriage of goods by sea, what is meant by (*a*) f.o.b., (*b*) c.i.f.? (**21**) [*N.C.T.E.C.*

12. What is the meaning of the following terms and abbreviations in connection with transport: (*a*) carriage forward, (*b*) carriage paid, (*c*) f.o.b., (*d*) c.i.f., (*e*) nt.wt., (*f*) B/L, (*g*) O.R., (*h*) C.O.D.? (**11, 21**)
[*U.E.I.*

CHAPTER VI

STOCK

1. Importance of stock control. Many businesses fail because inadequate attention is paid to stock control, which is important for the following reasons:

(*a*) Stock represents some of the capital of the business, and if too much is held the business may be short of cash.

(*b*) If too little is held, it may mean disappointed customers and a consequent loss of sales.

(*c*) In a manufacturing concern, stock control should be related to production, so that only those goods which are low in stock are manufactured and not the goods which are in plentiful supply and which may not be selling.

(*d*) Unless there is good stock control, stocks may be lost through damage or deterioration, or from pilfering.

(*e*) Stock control is linked with buying, and the purchasing department relies on accurate information from the stores department.

(*f*) Good stores staff ensure proper and prompt claims for damage, shortages or defects in goods received.

2. What is stock control? Stock control is concerned with the following functions:

(*a*) Receiving all goods purchased, checking, identifying and recording them, as well as reporting damage, shortages, etc.

(*b*) Storing stocks properly and in such a way that they can be easily located when required and so that they are kept in good condition.

(*c*) Making issues from stores as and when required, and only on the proper authority.

(*d*) Assisting in stock-taking at regular intervals (*see* **3** below).

(*e*) Keeping proper stock records of receipts and issues (*see* below).

(*f*) Making requests for re-ordering when stocks of any particular items are falling too low (*see* **10** below).

3. Stock-taking. Although stock records are kept, it is still necessary to take stock, *i.e.* the physical checking of all stocks on hand, because stock records (for various reasons: *see* **9** below) are rarely absolutely accurate.

Stock-taking involves the listing of every single item of stock with the quantities held, after which the items have to be individually priced and valued (*see* **8** below).

There are three main kinds of stock-taking:

(*a*) *Annual stock-taking*, which takes place at the end of a company's financial year, and is for the purpose of obtaining a valuation of stock for inclusion in the end-of-year final accounts.

(*b*) *Perpetual inventory* (*see* **5** below).

(*c*) *Periodic stock-taking*, as practised in the chain stores, where the manager is usually required to take stock every fortnight and return the figures to head office for valuation. With the large chain stores such as Woolworth's or Marks and Spencer's, total stocks at all branches will be worth millions of pounds, and the business cannot wait until the end of the year to assess which goods are not selling, or which goods have been stolen, so that a regular stock-taking every week or fortnight is essential.

4. Importance of stock-taking. Whichever method of stock-taking is used, there are several reasons for its importance:

(*a*) It serves as a check on the book figures shown in the books of account.

(*b*) It can assist in the detection of fraud and theft.

(*c*) It can inform management as to which of its goods are either over-stocked or under-stocked.

(*d*) It can reveal which stocks are deteriorating owing to the nature of the stock (*e.g.* iron goods becoming rusty) or to bad storage (*e.g.* goods becoming damp).

5. Perpetual inventory. This is the checking of small sections of stock at regular intervals throughout the year (perhaps once a month), so that during the year the whole of the stock is checked. It is important that any differences between the actual stocks counted and the stock books figures should be reported to management immediately. At the end of the year, the stock book figures (as corrected in the light of the perpetual inventory) are taken as the physical closing stock without further stock-taking.

6. Advantages of perpetual inventory.

(*a*) It avoids long and costly end-of-year stock-taking.
(*b*) Stock checks may be more thorough.
(*c*) Experienced staff can be employed on the stock check.
(*d*) It is not necessary to stop routine work to carry out the check.
(*e*) It has a salutary moral effect on the staff (*i.e.* it discourages pilfering).
(*f*) Excessive stocks or shortages can be discovered earlier than just at the end of the year.

7. Disadvantages of perpetual inventory.

(*a*) Stock book figures may not be accurate (when taken as end-of-year stock).
(*b*) It extends the worry of stock-taking continuously throughout the year.
(*c*) In a busy stores department, there would not be time to spare for it.
(*d*) It takes more time, in total, of the administrative staff.

8. Stock-taking procedure. The procedure for an end-of-year stock-taking will vary with the size of the concern and the goods in stock, but a typical procedure might well be as follows:

(*a*) Publication of a timetable specifying dates when the stock-take is to start and when it has to finish; allowance should be made for checking, pricing and extensions on stock lists.

(*b*) Allocation of responsibility for the stock-taking, and particularly who is to be in charge of it.

(*c*) A check to ensure that all bin cards (running records of each item of stock attached to every bin or container of stock) and stock records are entered up to date.

(*d*) Some indication of which goods should be excluded from the stock-taking (usually things like string, brown paper and cleaning materials).

(*e*) Instructions on the method to be employed (*e.g.* top rack in the storeroom or bay to be counted first, and work downwards from left to right).

(*f*) To what extent the stock count should be checked, and who should do it.

(*g*) Indication of the accepted ways of counting goods; *e.g.* nuts and bolts can be assessed by their weight.

(*h*) Instructions about entering on separate lists all goods received and issued while the stock-take is in progress.

(*i*) A clear sign to be entered on the bin cards when stock therein has been counted and entered on the stock lists.

(*j*) The preparation of a list of the differences (if any) between the stock-taking and the stock records.

9. Differences between stock-taking and stock records. It often happens that the figures revealed by the stock-taking are subsequently found to disagree with the stock records, and there should first be an investigation into the cases, after which, if the discrepancy cannot be rectified, a report should be sent to management.

Reasons for a discrepancy might be as follows:

(*a*) That goods received have not been entered in the stock records.

(*b*) More usually, that requisitions for goods issued have been mislaid and not entered on the stock records.

(*c*) That goods have been issued when urgently required without a requisition, or that goods have been stolen.

Sometimes (perhaps owing to misposting of requisitions in the stock records) the actual stock is greater than the book stock.

Whenever the stock-taking reveals the stock to be over or under the book figures shown in the stock records, the differences should be reported. Usually, a special printed form or a standard book (sometimes called the "stock unders and overs" book) is used, in which the discrepancies (after full investigation) must be entered and submitted to top management. Usually, the differences have to be priced and valued, so that their importance can be assessed, and the manager or the managing body may then sign the book, thus giving approval to the correction of the stock record to agree with the physical stock-taking.

10. Methods of stock valuation. There are several methods of valuing stock, and the method chosen can have a great effect on the resultant total:

(*a*) *Cost price.* By this method the stock is valued according to the price paid for the goods.

(*b*) *Average price.* A difficulty is that several purchases may have been made at different prices, and, since the remaining stock may consist of some of each delivery, an average price is calculated over the different purchases. This method involves a good deal of work.

(*c*) *Market price.* Since the real value of goods is what they will fetch on the market, they can be valued at present-day prices (usually, this is the price paid most recently).

(*d*) *Specific price.* Where goods are big and expensive, it may be necessary to identify them by the date of purchase and price them according to the specific price paid for each of them.

(*e*) *Cost or market price, whichever is the lower.* This is the method approved by the Board of Inland Revenue, and it means that if goods have fallen in value since they were purchased then they will be valued at the reduced amount, but if they have increased in value they will be valued at the purchase-price value.

11. Stock records. The basic stock record is, of course, the *stock book*, but in addition there will be *requisitions* where users indent for their withdrawals from stock, a *goods received book* (or goods received notes) and *bin cards* (*see* **8** above).

Typical stock records today will be in a visible card index form and will resemble Fig. 12 (note that a separate card is maintained for each item of stock). It will be seen that the stock record shows the date, the quantity of goods issued, and the date and quantity of goods received from time to time. The balance column has to be calculated afresh by the stock clerk every time an entry is made on the card.

Stock records are important for the following reasons:

(*a*) They enable the management to check on the stock of any item at any time.

(*b*) They draw attention to goods which are under-stocked and need replenishing.

(*c*) They draw attention to the over-stocking of goods

which are not now in use or which are used very slowly.

(d) They act as a check on the physical stock, particularly in an effort to prevent fraud and theft.

ITEM:						MINIMUM:
UNITS:						MAXIMUM:
RECEIVED			ISSUED			BALANCE
Date	G.R.N.No.	No.	Date	Req. No.	No.	

Fig. 12.—*Stock record.*

Is it better to have stock records maintained in a bound book or in the form of a visible card index? Generally speaking, the latter offers most advantages. Relative advantages of the two methods are as follows:

Bound books
(a) Contains all the stock records, and individual records cannot be mislaid or misfiled.
(b) Best for prevention of fraud.
(c) May be cheaper.

Visible card index
(a) Discontinued items of stock can be moved to a "discontinued" section.
(b) Records can be rearranged in any desired order.
(c) Coloured signals can be used on the edges of cards to draw attention to under- or overstocking or to goods awaiting delivery.
(d) No blank pages need be left for expansion.

(e) Easy to refer to a particular section of the stock records without disturbing the routine work.

(f) Speed of reference.

12. Replenishing stock. As mentioned above, one of the purposes of keeping stock records is to ensure that stocks are replenished as required. A business requires to carry sufficient stock of anything to run the business smoothly without being held up by shortage of materials, and yet it must not carry too much stock of any item, because this ties up capital that could be invested more profitably elsewhere.

In an effort therefore to guard against having too little stock or too much, it is usual to have entered on the stock records (*see* **10** above) two figures estimated to be:

(a) minimum stock and
(b) maximum stock.

Then it is the job of the stock record clerk to keep a constant watch on the balance column of the card and compare it constantly with the minimum and maximum figures entered at the top of the card. Immediately the current balance of stock of any item falls below the minimum, it must be reported to the supervisor, so that orders can be put in hand for fresh stock to be purchased of that item. Similarly, if the balance of any item is seriously above the maximum, it should also be reported.

13. Stock requisitions. Requisitions (sometimes called "indents") are printed forms on which the users of materials apply for the issue of stock. They are numbered and must be signed by some official authorised to sign them. Often they are prepared in quadruplicate:

(a) One goes to the stores department requesting the goods.

(b) A second goes to the stores department where it is marked to show whether the goods are available, etc., and then returned with the goods for checking.

(c) A third goes to the stock or costing department for entering in stock and/or costing records.

(*d*) A fourth remains the book of the department indenting for the goods.

STORES REQUISITION   No.

To the Storekeeper: please supply :-

Quantity	Cat. No.	Job	Price	Amount

Signed..............................

FIG. 13.—*Stock requisition.*
Only the first, second and third columns are completed by the drawer of the requisition.

An example of a stock requisition is shown in Fig. 13. It is essential that no goods should be issued from the stores department unless a properly signed requisition is presented for them.

14. Valuation of issues. Note that on the requisition shown in Fig. 13 there are columns for the pricing of goods and their values to be extended. Some businesses maintain records of quantities only on the stock records (as in **11** above) and have valued requisitions, so that the value of goods used can be charged to different jobs (this is an aspect of costing), while other firms keep valued stock records and valued requisitions, so that they can determine at any time not only the quantity of stock in hand of any item but also its value.

Where requisitions are valued, then, as with stock-taking, there are different methods of pricing the goods entered on them as follows:

(a) *FIFO* (*first in, first out*), sometimes called LILO (last in, last out), which means that it is assumed that the goods first received will be the first issued, so the issues are valued at the price paid for the first purchases made in the period.

(b) *FILO* (*first in, last out*), which means that goods issued are always valued at the prices paid for the last consignment bought.

(c) *List price*, which would generally be used only where invoices for goods received had not yet been received, so that the list price is used in the meantime.

(d) *Average cost price*, where all issues are priced at the average of prices paid during the period (since it is not known which goods have been issued first).

15. Special goods. Where a department requisitions for something which is not kept in stock, then the requisition concerned will be sent to the purchasing department, so that a special order can be placed for the goods required. Such goods (sometimes referred to as "specials") are not taken into stock, *i.e.* not entered on any stock records, since as soon as the goods are received they will be issued to the requisitioning department.

PROGRESS TEST 6

1. What is meant by continuous stock-taking? (**3**) [*U.L.C.I.*

2. Stock-taking in many organisations is carried out by means of the perpetual inventory system.

(a) How does this system operate?

(b) Are any benefits obtained by an organisation using this system as opposed to any other method that you know? (**3, 6**)

[*E.M.E.U.*

3. Explain how continuous stock-taking operates, and state its advantages and disadvantages as compared with other systems of stock-taking. (**3, 6, 7**) [*E.M.E.U.*

4. (a) It is customary for a business to value its stock in monetary terms once every year. Why is this done?

(b) Some companies value their stocks more frequently—as often perhaps as once a week. Why do you think they find this necessary?

(c) Mention two methods of valuing stock and say what kind of businesses might use them. (**3, 10**) [*R.S.A.*

5. A new employee in the stores department tells you that he cannot see why the firm goes to the trouble to take stock—it only wastes the time of people busy enough already. State how you would explain (a)

the reasons for taking stock and (b) the ways in which stock is valued for stock-taking purposes. Suggest any means of making the stock-taking burden easier. (4) [R.S.A.

6. What is the purpose of stock-taking? Explain what is meant by continuous stock-taking and state its advantages. (4) [Y.C.F.E.

7. (a) Why is it essential to take stock regularly?

(b) What use can be made of the information on a stock record card? (4, 11) [E.M.E.U.

8. Describe the procedure when an organisation has its annual stock-taking. (8) [N.C.T.E.C.

9. Stock records are important. Why? (11) [U.L.C.I.

10. When taking stock it is discovered that the physical amount of a certain item differs from the amount shown on the stock control records. State the possible reasons for this discrepancy and describe the procedure which you would follow in dealing with the matter. (9)

[U.E.I.

11. List the various methods of valuing stocks for the purpose of stock-taking and describe in full *two* of the methods indicating their relative advantages and disadvantages. (10) [U.E.I.

12. (a) What do the terms "maximum" and "minimum" mean when printed on a stock record card?

(b) Name and describe any methods of stock valuation that you know. (10, 12) [E.M.E.U.

13. You work for a small business which uses a bound book for keeping its stock records. There is a suggestion that a card system would be more appropriate.

You are required:

(a) to set out, in the form of a simple report, the advantages and disadvantages of bound books and cards for stock record purposes;

(b) to draft a card you think might be suitable. (11) [R.S.A.

14. Draft a stock sheet and enter two items as examples. (8)

[U.L.C.I.

15. Why is it necessary to maintain stock records? (11) [U.L.C.I.

16. Draw up a stock record card to deal with the control of foolscap duplicating paper which is supplied in packets of 500 sheets. (11)

[Y.C.F.E.

17. Design a stock record sheet and show how the following information would be recorded on it:

White line: 7lb bags; in stock March 1st 893 @ £0·05 £44·65.

Issued March 2nd 586 @ £0·05 £29·30; received March 5th 1,456 @ £0·05 £72·80 (11) [U.E.I.

18. How does a storekeeper (a) replenish his stocks of standard goods, (b) obtain special goods for a department? (12, 15)

[N.C.T.E.C.

19. Write brief notes on stores requisitions. (13) [N.C.T.E.C.

20. Draw a stores requisition slip and make suitable entries. Say how this document is used in business. **(13)** [*R.S.A.*

21. Describe a procedure to be followed in the requisitioning of stock. **(13)** [*U.L.C.I.*

22. The following articles were purchased by a firm:

Sept.	3	50 articles	£0·90 ea.	Sept.	16	50 articles	£0·85
	8	100 ,,	£0·85 ,,		24	50 ,,	£0·95
	10	100 ,,	£0·80 ,,		29	200 ,,	£0·80

400 articles were found to be in stock on 30th September. Work out the different values of the 400 articles using each of the following methods: (*a*) average cost price; (*b*) list price; (*c*) LILO; (*d*) FILO. **(14)**
[*U.E.I.*

CHAPTER VII
MONEY AND BANKING

1. Services of a bank. A bank is useful for personal reasons, but it is also very useful to business because it provides a number of services. The three main services provided by a bank are as follows:

(a) The *safekeeping of money* not immediately required (many businesses pay their cash into the bank every day).

(b) The granting of *loans and overdrafts* (usually only on a temporary basis, and provided some security is given to the bank, but not as long-term capital).

(c) The provision of *cheque facilities*, which make it much easier to settle debts than with large amounts of cash.

In addition, a bank also provides the following services which may or may not be used by individual business concerns:

(a) *Night safe*, whereby money can be deposited at the bank after closing hours by means of a posting box in the wall outside the bank. The money is put in a locked bag and when posted it falls down into the bank's underground safe.

(b) *Travellers' cheques and foreign currency*, which are of great use when foreign travel is anticipated (*see* **18** below).

(c) *Discounting bills of exchange*, in connection with trade with other countries (importing and exporting).

(d) *Safe facilities*, where a private person or business may keep valuable jewellery, important contracts, insurance policies, etc.

(e) *Executor or trustee:* if required, the bank will act as executor of a will for the purpose of administration of the estate of the deceased.

(f) *Investments:* the bank will advise and even make investments on behalf of its customers.

(g) *Status enquiries* for credit control: a bank will act as a reference when opening a credit account with another company.

(h) *Standing orders*, by which a bank will make regular

payments for hire purchase, rent, rates, etc., on behalf of its customers (*see* **19** below).

2. Types of bank account. There are two main types of account which can be maintained at a bank; one is called a *current account* and the other a *deposit account*.

(*a*) *A current account* is the normal account maintained by a customer, whether private or business, which is used in the normal day-to-day running of the business, *i.e.* for paying in and for the drawing out of money.

  (*i*) It is the account on which cheques can be drawn.
  (*ii*) The bank does not pay interest on money left in the current account.
  (*iii*) Bank charges are made by the bank for the running of the account; these vary with the amount of money kept in the account and the number of cheques drawn.

(*b*) *A deposit account* is a special account opened when there is surplus cash on the current account.

  (*i*) The bank gives interest on the amount kept in the deposit account.
  (*ii*) Cheques cannot be drawn on this account, although withdrawal of cash can be made on completion of a special form.
  (*iii*) Cash can be withdrawn only by giving a certain length of notice (usually at least seven days).
  (*iv*) No bank charges are made by the bank for keeping such an account.

3. Opening a bank account. To open a bank account, all that is required is to follow a standard procedure:

(*a*) Take a sum of money to the bank.
(*b*) Complete an application form.
(*c*) Give specimen signatures of the persons who will sign cheques.
(*d*) Quote references, so that the bank can verify that the applicant is of good standing.
(*e*) If a company, supply copies of Articles of Association, past balance sheets, etc.

Then the bank will issue a cheque book and a paying-in book, and in due course the account will be opened.

4. Advantages and disadvantages. The advantages of having a bank account are abundantly clear from the services provided in **1** above, and if there are any disadvantages these are peculiar to the kind of account maintained. Thus, bank charges have to be paid with a current account, and notice of withdrawal must be given with a deposit account. It can also be quoted that a current account gives no interest on money deposited (although a deposit account does). However, the advantages of having a bank account far outweigh the disadvantages.

5. Methods of payment. Methods of payment open to a business are many, and details only of those other than through the bank are given here, as payments through the bank are dealt with in detail subsequently.

(*a*) *By sending cash through the post.* Money should not be sent by ordinary letter post, because if it is lost, a claim for compensation is unlikely to succeed. The Post Office regulations state that money can be sent by registered post, provided that the special registered envelopes are used (or their equivalent), and that coins should not move about (they should be wrapped and secured with adhesive tape or a rubber band). The maximum compensation even with registered post is limited, so this method should be used only for small amounts of £1 or so.

(*b*) *By postal order.* Again, this method should be used only for small amounts, as poundage (the Post Office charge for issuing postal orders) is charged on every postal order according to its value. Currently, postal orders can be obtained for amounts from 5p to £1 and then in £1 steps up to £10. Stamps for odd pence can be affixed to increase the face value of a postal order. This is a useful method for remitting money to people who do not have a bank account.

(*c*) *By T.M.O.* (*telegraphic money order*). This is a method of remitting money by telegraph and is the quickest means of payment, but a standard charge has to be added to the cost of the telegram. Although this service is still in existence, ordinary money orders themselves have been discontinued.

(*d*) *By National Giro.* In effect, this is a banking service offered by the Post Office and, provided that the payee also has a Giro account, is the quickest method of payment. Provided that a minimum amount is held in the Giro account (at present £30), such payments can be made to another Giro account free of charge.

But, for Girocheques for payments of *cash* to someone without a Giro account, there is currently a charge of 10p per payment (plus a further 5p if there is less than £30 in the account of the Ordinary Account holder).

NOTE: No interest is given by the National Giro on money kept in a Giro account, but the Giro service does offer a relatively cheap means of payment. If an employer pays a person's salary direct to a Giro account, even more preferential terms are obtainable.

(*e*) *By cheque sent to the payee* (*see* **7** below).
(*f*) *By credit transfer* (*see* **11** below).

Legal tender can be defined as any means of payment which a debtor can legally compel his creditor to accept in settlement of a debt. Thus the maximum that can be tendered in settlement of a debt is: bronze coins (commonly called "copper") up to 20p; cupro-nickel (commonly called "silver") up to £5; and 50p pieces up to £10.

6. Documents involved with a bank account. When a bank account is opened, the usual documents involved (apart from the opening procedure) are the following:

(*a*) *Cheque book*, by means of which cash can be withdrawn from the bank and payments made to other people.

(*b*) *Paying-in book*, which is used to make payments into the bank account.

(*c*) *Bank statement*, which is the name given to the statement of account sent by the bank to the customer at regular intervals, to inform him of the state of his account.

(*d*) *Pass book*. In the case of a deposit account, a pass book may need to be produced every time deposits or withdrawals are made.

7. Cheques. A cheque is an order drawn on the bank, instructing it to make payment to the person (or business) named on the cheque, and for the sum of money specified.

When drawing a cheque, attention must be given to the following matters:

(*a*) That the cheque bears the correct date (if by mistake the 30th of a month was written instead of the 20th, the receiver of the cheque would not be able to receive payment until the 30th).

(*b*) That the cheque bears the correct name of the receiver

VII. MONEY AND BANKING 63

(*i.e.* the payee). The correct name in full can be obtained by referring to the letterheading used by the business. When paying an individual, "Mr" or "Mrs" is not necessary, although the full Christian name is preferable to just initials.

(*c*) That the amount of money is stated in writing, as well as in figures, and that they agree. Furthermore, to prevent fraud, the figures should be written with the amount in pounds hard up against the £ sign (*see* Fig. 14).

(*d*) That the cheque is signed by the proper person authorised to draw cheques on the bank account.

(*e*) That the cheque is crossed if this is required (*see* below).

It should be noted that the person who writes and signs a cheque is known as the "drawer" (he draws it on the bank); the person to whom it is payable is the "payee" (*i.e.* the person entitled to payment); and the bank on which it is drawn is the "drawee", who is charged with the duty of payment, since a cheque is an order to pay.

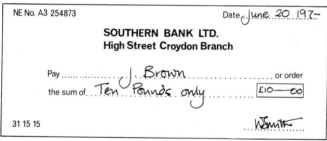

Fig. 14.—*Cheque.*

8. Open and crossed cheques.

(*a*) An *open cheque* is one which is without a crossing; this can be used:

  (*i*) to pay salaries (particularly for persons without bank accounts);
  (*ii*) for drawing cash from the bank;
  (*iii*) for paying money to another person (*e.g.* a customer) without a bank account.

Such a cheque can be cashed over the counter of the bank it is drawn on.

(*b*) A *crossed cheque* is one which has two parallel lines drawn across it and it may have "& Co" inside the lines, but this is traditional and is not necessary. This is called a "general crossing".

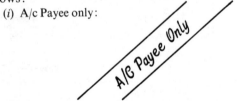

The effect of the crossing is that it can be paid only into a bank account (or Post Office National Savings or National Giro account); *i.e.* it cannot be exchanged for cash. It therefore offers greater security, because if it is lost or stolen it cannot be exchanged for cash but only paid into another bank account.

However, with a general crossing, it is possible for the payee to negotiate (*i.e.* transfer) payment of the cheque to another party. This is performed by the payee writing on the back of the cheque "Pay A. Blogg, J. Smith" (*i.e.* if the cheque is payable to J. Smith).

(*c*) *Types of crossing.* Some types of crossing (special crossings) in addition to the simple crossing shown above are as follows:

(*i*) A/c Payee only:

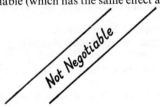

This has the effect of making the cheque payable only to the bank account of the person named on the cheque; *i.e.* it is not possible for the payee to transfer (negotiate) payment to any other person.

(*ii*) Not negotiable (which has the same effect as (*i*)):

(*iii*) *Specific banks crossings* are where, as a further safety precaution, the name of a specific bank is inserted in the crossing, which makes the cheque payable into the account of the payee only at the bank (and perhaps the particular branch) mentioned in the crossing:

9. Advantages and disadvantages of paying by cheque.

(*a*) *Advantages* include *convenience*, because it is easy to write a cheque at any time, and *safety* (if it is crossed), because it can be paid only into a bank account. It also saves a businessman from having to carry large sums of money around and offers a quick means of payment because a cheque can be put in the post and the payee can pay it into his bank account within a day or so.

(*b*) *Disadvantages* include the fact that it is necessary to have a bank account with sums of money in it not earning interest; that the more cheques drawn the higher are the bank charges; that the payee might have difficulty in cashing a cheque if he does not have a bank account; and that when it is not crossed it can be stolen and cashed in the same way as money.

NOTE: When the payee does not have an account at the bank into which to pay a crossed cheque, he can either pay it into a Post Office National Savings account or negotiate it to a tradesman with whom he is on friendly terms who will give the payee cash and pay it into his own bank account. Not all tradesmen will oblige in this way, however, because they are taking a chance on whether the cheque is a good one (*see* **14** on dishonoured cheques).

10. Personal cheques, bank draft, dividend warrant.

(*a*) *Personal cheques*. To encourage the public to make use of banking services even without opening a bank account, some banks offer a personal cheque service, which means that an individual cheque can be obtained at a bank in exchange for the amount of cash mentioned on the cheque, plus a small charge.

(b) *Bank draft (or warrant).* This is used mostly in transactions which require a high degree of certainty of payment, and is used widely in overseas trade, where a foreigner may be unaware of the financial standing of the other party to the transaction. On the application of the party making payment, his bank issues a "cheque" drawn on itself (*i.e.* the bank is both drawer and drawee) which is therefore virtually certain to be honoured.

(c) *Marked cheque.* When taking payment for a large sum of money inside the country and the payee is not sure whether the cheque is a good one (*i.e.* if the drawer has sufficient cash to meet the cheque), very often the seller of expensive goods (such as a car) will demand a three-day waiting period before releasing the goods being bought, in order that the cheque can be "cleared" (*i.e.* charged to the drawer's account).

To meet this difficulty, the drawer of a cheque can get the bank to mark on the cheque that it will be met (*i.e.* that sufficient funds are kept at the bank to meet it). The cheque will then be accepted immediately by the seller of the goods, and the goods will be released without delay.

(d) *Dividend warrant* is the name given to a document sent to shareholders for the dividend due to them on account of their shareholdings. It is equivalent to a cheque, and can be paid into the bank in the same way as a cheque.

11. Credit transfer.

(a) A common use for credit transfer is for the payment of salaries in a large undertaking, and it represents a method of payment whereby the payer completes, for each payee, separate forms on which he designates the payee's name, bank and bank account number, and the amount of money being paid. These forms (*see* Fig. 15) are accompanied by a summary of them and *one cheque for the total* is then passed to the bank, which then transfers the sums of money from the payer's account direct to the various accounts of the payees. It avoids the need for drawing large numbers of cheques, it offers even greater security than payment by individual cheques and it saves in office work since the credit transfer forms can be prepared by various office machines.

```
┌─────────────────────────────────────────────┐
│ Southern Bank Limited                       │
│ CREDIT TRANSFER                             │
│ Date....................  Code No...................   │
│             To                              │
│             Bank..........................................│
│             Branch........................................│
│                                        £.................. │
│             ..........................................│
│             ACCOUNT......................................│
│             Paid in by....................................│
└─────────────────────────────────────────────┘
```

Fig. 15.—*Credit transfer.*

(*b*) Credit transfer also offers a means of payment for people without a bank account, for if the relevant form is completed and taken to a bank with the required sum of money, plus a small charge (bank charge), such amount will then be transferred to the account designated on the form.

An example of a credit transfer summary form, which accompanies the individual credit transfer forms sent to the bank, is shown in Fig. 16.

To SOUTHERN BANK LTD.	....................................Address
.... Branch	Date...........................
	Sheet No......................

Please distribute the attached credits as arranged with the recipients.

Our cheque for £.................. is enclosed.

....
(Authorised Signatories)

CODE	BANK AND BRANCH	FOR ACCOUNT OF	AMOUNT

Fig. 16.—*Credit transfer summary form.*

12. Credit cards. At least one national bank is well known for its bank credit card system, by which the customer is issued with a card (usually an embossed plastic plate in fact) by which he can obtain goods on credit up to the value of £200 at a time at designated suppliers (the bank concerned having previously made arrangements with such suppliers to accept payment by the production of such cards). The amounts of money spent by this means are then debited to the customer's credit card account.

The system has the advantage of dispensing with the need for carrying a cheque book, but it restricts the use of such cards to the designated suppliers, while cheques are universally acceptable. Such cards can be useful if one is travelling widely in the U.K., but it can be very inconvenient if the card is mislaid.

Similar credit card facilities are provided by private concerns for buying on credit from certain shops and then settling the account subsequently—usually the following month.

13. Bank cheque cards. Because some shopkeepers have been defrauded by accepting worthless cheques, most commercial banks issue their customers with cheque cards. When such a card is presented with a cheque in payment for goods purchased, it guarantees to the shopkeeper that the cheque will be paid by the bank—usually subject to a maximum of £30.

This is not the same as a credit card, for goods cannot be purchased with it alone, although it can be used in the same way as a credit card for the drawing of cash at designated banks.

14. Lost cheques. When cheques are lost (perhaps in the post) it is necessary to take the following action:

(*a*) Make enquiry of the Post Office in an endeavour to trace the missing letter.

(*b*) Inform the bank to stop payment of the cheque (*i.e.* if it has not already been presented).

(*c*) Apologise to the payee and *in due course* (*i.e.* after (*a*) and (*b*)) draw another cheque, because the debt is still in existence and still has to be settled.

15. R/D (dishonoured) cheques. For certain reasons, a bank may refuse to make payment of a cheque, and will return it to the payee marked "R/D" ("refer to drawer"), which indicates that the payee should refer to the drawer of the cheque for the reason why it cannot be met.

The reason for such an occurrence may be one of the following:

(*a*) That there are insufficient funds at the bank to meet the cheque.

(*b*) That the cheque is not signed (or not signed correctly).

(*c*) That the cheque bears the wrong date (*see* **16** below).

(*d*) That there is a disagreement in the writing and the figures as to the sum of money being paid.

Usually, a fresh cheque which is acceptable to the bank must be drawn and sent to the payee.

16. Post-dated cheques. When the drawer of a cheque has insufficient funds to meet the amount of the cheque but expects to have sufficient in the future (or when he purposely wishes to delay payment), he may date the cheque in advance of the date of drawing it. Thus, if it is drawn on the 20th of the month, it might be dated the 31st.

The effect of this is that the bank will refuse to pay the cheque, *i.e.* if it is presented to the bank immediately on receipt by the payee. Knowing this, most business concerns will refuse to accept a post-dated cheque because it only means that they have to keep it in their office safe until the date of the cheque arrives; in other words they do not receive payment until that date.

17. Stale cheques. A stale cheque is one which is more than six months old. In the banking world, this is the accepted practice, although it does not mean that because of its age such a cheque will not be accepted.

The effect of presenting a stale cheque to the bank is that the bank will enquire of the drawer whether it is still in order and, if assured that it is correct, will credit the payee's account just the same as if it were not stale.

18. Travellers' cheques. Travellers' cheques are issued by banks for the convenience of customers who are going to be away from home for a long period and wish to obtain sums of cash or make payments to strangers who would not accept personal cheques.

They are particularly useful when travelling abroad, and they are always acceptable at other banks because in effect they have the backing of the bank of issue. Usually, they are in standard denominations of £2, £5, £10, £20, etc., and can be cashed at any bank, with agents or even at hotels.

It is important that travellers' cheques should be signed immediately they are received, because if stolen they can easily be cashed by inserting false signatures.

19. Standing orders. A standing order is an order given to the bank to pay a fixed sum of money at regular intervals from one's bank account to a designated payee.

Thus building society payments, hire purchase payments, etc., may be paid monthly and subscriptions to professional societies may be paid yearly by this method.

The advantages of using standing orders for such payments are that it saves the repeated drawing of cheques and spending money on stationery and postage, as well as making certain that the payments are made on the due dates.

If there are any disadvantages, they are that the bank may make charges for the provision of such a service and that, when a person is calculating the amount in credit at the bank, allowance must be made for payments made by standing orders, which are easily forgotten.

20. Paying in to a bank. Every time a deposit (whether cash or cheques) is made at the bank, a form known as a "paying-in slip" has to be completed and signed by the person making the deposit (*see* Fig. 17). For this purpose, the bank supplies a paying-in book, which is a number of these forms bound together, although should this book not be available there are usually loose paying-in slips on the counter of the bank for the use of customers.

The paying-in slip must be dated and should show details of the notes, coins and cheques paid in, and must be completed in duplicate, one copy of which is retained by the bank and the other rubber-stamped by the bank and initialled by the bank clerk, thus constituting a receipt and evidence that the money has been paid to the bank.

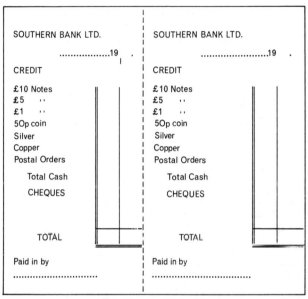

Fig. 17.—*Paying-in slip*.

When one is paying in money to a deposit account, a different form is used, and the pass book must be produced.

21. Bank statement. At regular intervals (depending on the number of transactions in the account) the bank supplies every customer with a bank statement, which is a statement of the customer's account as it appears in the bank's ledger. It usually begins with a balance brought forward from the previous statement, and then lists, with dates and means of identification, all the credits (amounts paid in) and all the debits (cheques drawn and charges made by the bank) in the period covered.

The customer should check the bank statement with the cheque book and paying-in book to see that it is correct, but allowance must be made for the following.

(*a*) Bank charges, which are not notified to the customer and can be learned only from the statement.

(*b*) Cheques drawn and not presented by the payees at the date of the statement.

(c) Cheques paid in, but not credited to the account by the date of the statement (some might be paid in at distant banks and take a few days to reach the bank holding the account).

PROGRESS TEST 7

1. List the services provided by a bank. Describe briefly *four* of the services listed. (**1**) [*U.L.C.I.*

2. Explain how a current account is opened. How is it used? (**2, 3**) [*Y.C.F.E.*

3. Explain the difference between a current account and a deposit account, and state with reasons which of these two accounts is likely to be maintained by a business firm. (**2**) [*U.E.I.*

4. Your firm has opened a branch in a small town and wishes to open a bank account.

(*a*) If you were instructed to do this, what action would you take?

(*b*) Draft *either* a cheque form *or* a paying-in slip, and make specimen entries. (**3, 7, 20**) [*R.S.A.*

5. Give a short description of the methods provided by the Post Office for the transfer of money. (**5**) [*U.L.C.I.*

6. Discuss briefly the various methods that are available to a trading organisation for settling its accounts. (**5**) [*E.M.E.U.*

7. Compare telegraphic money orders and postal orders as means of transferring money. (**5**) [*N.C.T.E.C.*

8. In what circumstances would each of the following be used as a means of payment: (*a*) bank warrant, (*b*) dividend warrant, (*c*) a crossed cheque, (*d*) a postal order? (**5, 8, 10**) [*Y.C.F.E.*

9. (*a*) What are the principal points to be borne in mind when drawing a cheque? What is (*i*) the object and (*ii*) the effect of crossing a cheque?

(*b*) What additions may be made to a cheque by a person other than the drawer without invalidating it? (**7, 8**) [*U.E.I.*

10. Who are (*a*) the drawer, and (*b*) the payee of a cheque? Why is the cheque preferred by business for making payment? (**8, 9**) [*U.E.I.*

11. Explain the meaning of the following crossings on cheques: (*a*) & Co., (*b*) Westminster Bank, (*c*) Account payee only, (*d*) Under ten pounds. (**8**) [*U.L.C.I.*

12. (*a*) When drawing a cheque, how can you ensure that it be paid only into the payee's account at a specific bank?

(*b*) List some of the benefits that the businessman gets by using his bank's credit transfer service.

(*c*) For what purposes might your firm use an open cheque? (**8, 11**) [*E.M.E.U.*

13. (*a*) Explain how the credit transfer system operates for settling accounts.

(b) What is the significance of a crossed cheque?

(c) Describe two types of special crossing that might be found on a cheque. **(8, 11)** [*E.M.E.U.*

14. (a) What is the purpose of crossing a cheque?

(b) A cheque posted by your firm to T. Smith has not been received by him. What action would you take? **(8, 14)** [*Y.C.F.E.*

15. Smith, who is employed by your firm and has no bank account, approaches you for advice. He has received a cheque for £10 drawn in his favour on the Midland Bank Ltd., Leek, from a Mr Brown. Advise him how he can get payment if:

(a) it is an open/bearer cheque;

(b) it is crossed and to his order; or

(c) it is specially crossed "Lloyds Bank, Lichfield." **(8, 9)** [*U.E.I.*

16. Explain the following terms: (a) a dishonoured cheque, (b) a post-dated cheque, (c) a crossed cheque. **(8, 15, 16)** [*W.J.E.C.*

17. List as many different methods as you can of withdrawing money from a bank account. Write a brief account of each, indicating its particular use to the bank's customer. **(8, 10, 11, 12, 19)** [*R.S.A.*

18. Describe the use of cheques and of credit cards as a means of settling debts, showing the advantages and disadvantages of each. **(9, 12)** [*E.M.E.U.*

19. (a) How is money transferred by credit transfer?

(b) What are personal cheques and how do they differ from other cheques? **(10, 11)** [*N.C.T.E.C.*

20. Write brief notes on the following business documents: (a) bank statement, (b) dividend warrant, (c) petty cash voucher. **(10, 11)**
[*N.C.T.E.C.*

21. The AB Company paid the following amounts by bank credit transfer from the Middleton Bank:

£147·55 to W. Jones   £198·60 to A. Zeal
£118·80 to L. Right   £175·50 to W. Brown
£132·75 to T. Light   £144·10 to C. Green

Draft the bank credit transfer list for these payments, and say how much will remain in the AB Company's current account if the previous balance was £1,500. **(11)** [*U.L.C.I.*

22. What is the credit transfer service? Explain its operation. **(11)**
[*Y.C.F.E.*

23. What are the uses of a bank credit card? **(12)** [*U.L.C.I.*

24. Your managing director frequently travels on business, and he wants to avoid having to carry large sums of cash to meet expenses. What facilities would you suggest to him? **(12, 18))** [*Y.C.F.E.*

25. What are banker's orders, and for what purposes are they used? **(19)** [*W.J.E.C.*

26. Explain the following terms: (a) bank statement; (b) standing order. **(19, 21)** [*Y.C.F.E.*

CHAPTER VIII

PETTY CASH

1. Cash book and petty-cash book. Most businesses pay for nearly everything by cheque, and receive either cheques or cash from customers, which they pay into the bank. These payments *from* the bank account and payments *in* are recorded in the main *cash book* of the company, which forms an integral part of the system of accounting.

However, in every business, there is a need to have ready cash in the office at all times to meet the small items of expenditure such as office tea, milk and sugar, flowers for the managing director's desk, bus and taxi fares, etc.

This money kept in the office is known as the "petty cash", and the book in which a record is kept of the receipts and payments from such fund is known as the *petty-cash book* (*see* Fig. 18).

2. Purposes of petty-cash book.

(*a*) Obviously, the first purpose of keeping such a book is to keep a record of receipts and payments from petty cash so that the difference (or balance) agrees with the amount of cash in hand.

Usually, the person keeping the petty-cash book has to take it at regular intervals (say once a week) to the firm's cashier for checking and verification that it "balances", *i.e.* that the amount of petty cash left in hand agrees with the balance stated in the book.

(*b*) It is usually kept in an analytical form so that the expenses can be automatically analysed while they are entered in the book (*see* below) and so that the totals of the different headings of expenditure can be posted (charged) to the appropriate accounts.

(*c*) It can also be viewed as a means of control over how the petty cash is spent—how much is spent on flowers, office tea, etc., each week or each month.

VIII. PETTY CASH

PETTY CASH BOOK

Cr. RECEIVED			PAID								Cr.
Date	Fo.	Amount	Date	Details	Voucher No.	Amount	Travelling	Postage	P. and S.	Sundries	
Jan. 1	384	20.00	Jan. 1	Fares	1	0.15	0.15				
			3	Stamps	2	2.00		2.00			
				Pins	3	0.15			0.15		
			5	Tips	4	0.25				0.25	
				Fares	5	0.30	0.30				
			7	Flowers	6	0.50				0.50	
						3.35	0.45	2.00	0.15	0.75	
		20.00		Balance c/d		16.65					
						20.00					
Jan. 8	b/d	16.65									
" 8	395	3.35									

FIG. 18.—*Petty-cash book*.

(a) "P. and S." stands for *printing and stationery*.
(b) "Fo." stands for *folio*, which indicates the relevant page in the firm's cash book.
(c) The total of the expenditure columns must equal the total of the daily figures.
(d) £3·35 in the Amount Received column is the reimbursement of the expenditure at the end of the week, which thus restores the original imprest of £20.

3. Principles of keeping the petty-cash book.

(*a*) The first basic principle is that there must be written proof of every item of expenditure, such as a receipted invoice or a petty-cash voucher (*see* below). Even bus tickets are required as evidence of fares paid.

(*b*) Some firms also have a rule that every item entered in the petty-cash book (and, of course, paid out) must be authorised and bear the signature of certain specified officials.

(*c*) Similarly, there is often a fixed list of expenses which can be paid from petty cash (to avoid its misuse). Examples of such expenditure are:

  (*i*) telegrams;
  (*ii*) carriage;
  (*iii*) travelling expenses;
  (*iv*) stationery (special small items);
  (*v*) office teas;
  (*vi*) entertaining;
  (*vii*) tips and gratuities;
  (*viii*) window cleaning.

Some firms even pay office cleaners through petty cash, and others allow quite large sums of cash to be withdrawn by company directors for business purposes.

(*d*) To make it easy to locate petty-cash vouchers, and so that auditors can check the entries, every voucher is given a serial number; these are usually numbered afresh each financial year.

4. Imprest system.

The imprest system is the usual method of keeping a petty-cash book, and it involves two operations:

(*a*) The advance of a round sum of money (say £20) sufficient to last for (say) a week.

(*b*) At the end of that period, and when the petty-cash book is checked, the reimbursement of the petty cash by an amount of cash equivalent to the total of expenditure in the period, thus restoring the amount of imprest advanced at the beginning.

This system has the advantage of making it easy to check the petty-cash book and deters fraud and theft.

5. Petty-cash vouchers.

Printed petty-cash vouchers are used, on which can be entered the details of the expenditure, the reasons for it, and by whom it is authorised (*see* Fig. 19).

```
+---------------------------------------------------------------+
|                 PETTY  CASH  VOUCHER          No........      |
|                                               Date.............|
|                                                               |
| PAY TO:                                                       |
| FOR                                                           |
|                                               Amount: £       |
| SIGNATURE.........................         Authorised by...........|
+---------------------------------------------------------------+
```

FIG. 19.—*Petty-cash voucher.*

PROGRESS TEST 8

1. State briefly the purposes of the following books, and name the department in which each is likely to be used:

(*a*) Cash book.
(*b*) Petty-cash book. (**1**) [*R.S.A.*

2. Describe a petty-cash book and a post book. (**1, 2**) [*U.L.C.I.*

3. (*a*) Name six different kinds of payment which are commonly made through petty cash.

(*b*) Describe how a petty-cash system operates. (**3**) [*N.C.T.E.C.*

4. Describe a system of keeping, and of accounting for, a sum of petty cash. (**4**) [*N.C.T.E.C.*

5. What is the petty-cash imprest system, and why is it used? (**4**) [*U.L.C.I.*

6. What is petty cash? Design an analysed petty-cash book and make six specimen entries. Explain how the imprest system works. (**3, 4**) [*Y.C.F.E.*

7. Draft a form of petty-cash voucher. (**5**) [*U.L.C.I.*

8. Draw a petty-cash voucher and make suitable entries. Say **how** this document is used in business. (**5**) [*R.S.A.*

CHAPTER IX

THE ACCOUNTANT'S DEPARTMENT

1. The <u>accountant's department</u> and <u>accounts section</u>. A list of functions of the accountant of a business was included in Chapter III, but a separate section of the accountant's department is sometimes called the *accounts section*. In this section are maintained the <u>customers' accounts</u> (or <u>Sales Ledger section</u>), and of course it forms a part of the main accounting section.

The function of the accounts section then is to maintain customers' ledger accounts, and to post to them all goods sold, as well as all cash received from customers, and <u>to send out monthly statements</u>, which are reminders and requests for the amounts due to the company.

2. Relationship with other departments. The accountant's department is a most important part of a business because it exercises financial control over the business and by its annual accounts (Profit and Loss Account and Balance Sheet) reveals how much profit the business is making.

Because the accountant's department is concerned with money, it is thus related in its working with every other department in the business:

(*a*) *With the sales department.* The accountant's department keeps records of the customers' ledger accounts, and exercises credit control over them to see that goods are not sold at the expense of bad debts.

(*b*) *With the personnel department.* Whatever extra staff or extra salaries and wages the personnel department might wish to recommend, it must be in accordance with what the business can afford.

(*c*) *With the company secretary's department.* The annual accounts (mentioned above) have to be submitted by the company secretary to the chairman, who in turn presents them to the shareholders at the annual general meeting.

(*d*) *With the purchasing department.* By the use of budgets of expenditure under different headings for the year, the accountant's department lays down how much can be spent on different items by the purchasing department.

(*e*) *With the works manager.* In a manufacturing company, the accountant's department will provide detailed costings of all processes, jobs or contracts, with the aim of increasing control and profitability.

3. Professional audit. Every company is required by law to engage professional accountants (that means accountants practising outside the business) for the purpose of carrying out an annual audit before the final accounts are placed before the shareholders.

The purpose of this audit is to safeguard the interest of the shareholders and to certify that the year-end final accounts do in fact give a true and accurate view of the financial affairs of the company.

These external auditors often take weeks or even months over the job of checking the company's books (depending on the size of the company), and for their services are paid large sums of money in professional fees, so it is advisable to give them every assistance on their annual visit to the company.

4. Internal audit. Some companies maintain their own internal audit section (of the accountant's department), which has really nothing to do with the external audit.

The staff of the internal audit section are employees of the company who maintain a continuous audit (check) of the books and records of the company (particularly where cash is concerned) with the object of preventing fraud as well as of making recommendations for improving the efficiency of the office systems in use.

5. Purchases: accounting routine. There is no standard system for dealing with purchase invoices (*i.e.* invoices received for goods purchased), but a system usually includes the following:

(*a*) As the purchase invoices are received, they are all filed alphabetically by the names of the companies from whom the goods have been purchased.

(*b*) As the goods are received, details of them are entered in a goods received book, or on to separate goods received notes. These are numbered, dated and filed in date order.

(c) Copies of all official orders for goods are usually sent to the accountant's department (from the purchasing department).

(d) Each day, purchase invoices received must be checked:

(i) against the official orders, checking quantities, descriptions, prices and trade discounts (the order number is then entered on the invoice);

(ii) with the goods received notes, checking quantities and descriptions and making claims for damaged goods, or shortages, etc. (then the goods received note number is also entered on the invoice).

(e) The invoices are rubber-stamped and initialled at each stage of the checking process.

(f) At regular intervals (say once a month) the monthly statements are compared with the cleared invoices and forwarded for payment (all cash discounts being claimed).

(g) The various invoices for the different firms are collated in date order, with the monthly statement on the top, and a cheque for the total is then prepared by the firm's cashier and the whole presented to the board of directors for signature.

PROGRESS TEST 9

1. What is the relationship of the accountant's department with the accounts section? (**1**)

2. Describe the relationship of the accountant's department with other departments in a business. (**2**)

3. What is meant by the annual audit and why is it necessary. (**3**)
[*U.L.C.I.*

4. What are the differences between the annual audit and the internal audit section of a business? (**3, 4**)

5. Describe the clerical procedure that would follow from the receipt by your stores of a consignment of previously ordered raw materials to the final payment being made to the supplier. (**5**)
[*E.M.E.U.*

NOTE: The questions not followed by initials of examining bodies are suggested questions only.

PART TWO

CLERICAL SERVICES

CHAPTER X

THE OFFICE

1. The relation of the office to the business. All business organisations and other institutions (such as hospitals) have offices, and, in fact, in some businesses (such as banking) the work done in the office is their sole function.

By *the office* is meant any office, and all offices in a business. In relation to the business as a whole the office may be said to have the following roles:

(*a*) *Secondary*. The main purpose of a business is to make a profit so that it can stay in existence. To do this, it usually trades (*i.e.* buys and sells goods), and since this is its main purpose all office work must be secondary to this purpose.

(*b*) *Complementary*. This means that office work is a necessary complement to the main purpose of the business which could not be achieved without office work. Thus, a factory needs raw materials in order to make its products, and the buying office will see that raw materials are purchased in the right quantity and at the right time. The workers in a factory will want wages every week, and the wages office calculates the amounts of pay and pays out the wages. There is little use in a factory making goods unless they can be sold, and the sales office arranges advertising and the selling of the goods produced.

(*c*) *Controlling*. The office exercises various controls over many aspects of the business. Perhaps the most important control is financial control exercised by the accountant's or cost accounting office. This means that they check on the amount of profit being made and whether it is sufficient, and on the amount of capital (and cash) kept in the company's bank account, and so on.

2. Office functions. The office does not usually produce any goods itself, and can be said to be non-productive (*i.e.* in comparison with a factory), but *it does produce services*, which can be stated as the following:

(*a*) *Communication:*

(*i*) *Receiving information* (about prices, orders for goods, applications for employment, etc.).

(*ii*) *Giving information* (prices to customers, orders for materials, etc.). A great deal of office work is concerned with giving information to management, by which the latter exercises control (*see* **1** (*c*) above) over finance, stock, labour employed, etc. A great value of an electronic computer is in its speed in giving information so that management is helped in making business decisions and exercising control.

(*b*) *Record:*

(*i*) *Keeping records* of all kinds about business activities such as stock, cash and sales.

(*ii*) *Arranging information* in a form which is suitable to management. Thus, costing involves a great deal of analysis of costs of production, and providing management with the analysed information.

An easy-to-remember guide to the basic functions of an office is R.R.A.G., which stands for "Recording, Receiving, Arranging and Giving information."

It must be remembered that the office provides a service; *e.g.* a training officer of a large enterprise will provide a service to top management in arranging training (as well as keeping records, etc.), and an advertising department will provide a service in arranging publicity for the company's goods.

NOTE: Some businesses, however, are of such a nature that *all* the work of the business is done in the office. Thus professional accountants, solicitors, insurance agents, etc., are themselves service industries to the rest of the commercial world.

An outstanding example is the case of a bank, where the work is concerned with safeguarding the cash of businesses and dealing with cheques, etc. Here, the office work performed is not secondary, for by keeping records, etc., the clerical work performed is basic to the whole purpose of the business.

X. THE OFFICE

3. Office work. The actual work performed in offices (as distinct from the function of the office) is very varied, but it can briefly be classified as follows:

(a) *Communicating* or transmitting information. This is performed by means of the telephone, letter-writing, etc.

(b) *Writing* or recording information, such as on stock records, sales records, etc. Many machines can be used to assist this aspect, such as the typewriter, addressing machine, etc.

(c) *Sorting* or arranging in classes, so that orders from customers may be sorted according to the degree of urgency, outgoing letters sorted according to the denomination of stamp required, etc.

(d) *Copying*, which involves, firstly, the copying of figures from a document on to a record or in a book. Thus, sales from customers are copied into a ledger to record how much money they owe for goods supplied. Secondly, copying may be the reproduction of one copy of a document (as with a photocopier) or the reproduction of 100 or 1,000 copies of a price list (as with an office duplicator).

(e) *Checking* or comparing one document with another. A great deal of checking is necessary in an office to ensure accuracy, for a single mistake (say in a purchase order) could cost the company thousands of pounds.

(f) *Calculating* or computing. The basic arithmetical processes of addition, subtraction, multiplication and division are mostly used, and various machines such as adding and calculating machines can be employed for this operation.

(g) *Filing* or the arranging and storing of documents so that they can be found when required. It is little use recording information unless it can be found when wanted, and there are often files relating to correspondence, to orders, to contracts, to applications for employment and so on.

4. Office work requirements.

From the foregoing, the knowledge and skills required of office workers will be apparent, but they will vary according to the department, with the individual job, and with the age and position of the staff.

(a) *Qualities* required of office workers include self-discipline (*e.g.* good timekeeping), patience (particularly with routine jobs and on the telephone), a sense of judgment (not speaking out of turn in the presence of superiors), the ability to be methodical and orderly in working habits, the ability to be precise and accurate (but not over-precise when it is not important) and the ability to get on with other people (with older people and people of the opposite sex or of a different race).

(b) *Knowledge* required will include a knowledge of the background to the business world, of the organisation of a business, of the functions of different departments, of the systems in use for different purposes, of different machines used in modern offices, of personnel practices and, in fact, of everything dealt with in this book.

(c) *Skills* required include the ability to operate simple office machines, to fill in forms, to file accurately, and to be able to sort and collate papers as required and by the quickest methods.

PROGRESS TEST 10

1. What is the function of the office in a business organisation? (**1**)
[*U.L.C.I.*

2. All business organisations and institutions (*e.g.* hospitals and colleges) have offices. Describe the clerical functions that these are likely to have in common. (**2**) [*R.S.A.*

3. What qualities, knowledge and skills do you consider a clerical worker should possess or develop? (**4**) [*U.L.C.I.*

CHAPTER XI

OFFICE COMMUNICATIONS

1. Methods of communication. Office communications are important because they are the means of representing the business to customers and to the public, and good internal communications represent one of the primary functions of the office. The wages office needs to communicate with the cashier, the costing department with the production department, and so on. Work in different offices could not progress without good communications. The different methods of communication are as follows:

(*a*) *Oral:* which, apart from personal, face-to-face conversations, are represented by telephone systems.

(*b*) *Written:* letter-writing and reporting, and the methods of transmitting written messages including the teleprinter and Telex.

(*c*) *Mechanical:* such as conveyor belts, lifts, etc.

(*d*) *Pictorial:* whereby pictures can be transmitted such as by closed circuit television or facsimile telegraphy.

(*e*) *Personal messengers:* many businesses have internal messenger services.

2. Telephone systems.

(*a*) A small business may have a *house exchange system* rented from the Post Office where there are up to five or ten extensions and one or two lines to the exchange. No switchboard is necessary, although some switching device is provided on the master instrument for routing incoming calls to different extensions.

(*b*) When a business grows beyond a certain size (perhaps requiring more than ten extensions) it can install a switchboard, and the system may be either of the following:

(*i*) *P.M.B.X.* (Private Manual Branch Exchange) where the switchboard operator makes connections for outgoing calls as well as incoming calls.

(*ii*) *P.A.B.X.* (Private Automatic Branch Exchange) where the extensions by dialling "9" receive the dialling tone and can then dial their own outgoing calls, as well as being able to dial other offices.

(c) In addition to these systems rented from the Post Office, a business may have its own internal house telephone which is not connected to the exchange, and by which other offices can be obtained by dialling or press-button. This is often referred to as the "intercom".

3. P.A.B.X. versus P.M.B.X. The usual choice in equipment is between a P.A.B.X. (where inter-office communication can be dialled) and a P.M.B.X. plus an internal house telephone.

(a) *Advantages of P.A.B.X.*

(i) Only one telephone on the desk is necessary.

(ii) It does not require as many telephone operators as a P.M.B.X. (in a big business concern).

(iii) It is most convenient to the users.

(iv) It avoids the dilemma which may occur when two telephones (P.M.B.X. and house telephone) on a desk are both ringing and need to be answered simultaneously.

(v) It reduces the amount of noise in an office.

(b) *Advantages of P.M.B.X. and house telephone.*

(i) It is often useful when receiving a call on the "outside" line to be able to contact another department, while still holding the outside line (particularly useful when wishing to transfer a call to another department).

(ii) When offices do not make many calls outside the firm, it is more economic to provide only internal telephones.

(iii) It means that the outside lines are not clogged with inter-office calls, and that customers are not annoyed by being kept waiting for long periods.

(iv) It may be cheaper in telephone rentals.

4. Telephone operating. Business firms prefer to recruit telephone operators from those who have had Post Office training because it means they have had good tuition, whereas many telephone operators have just learned the job by acting as relief, perhaps at lunch-times and during holidays.

A good telephone operator requires the following qualities:

(a) A good speaking voice and diction.

(b) A pleasant and courteous personality.

(c) A great deal of patience.

(d) Technical competence, *i.e.* a knowledge of all matters

pertaining to the telephone service.

(*e*) Tact, particularly when speaking to irate, difficult members of the public, or when dealing with the management.

(*f*) A good memory.

(*g*) Good handwriting (she often has to keep a record of calls made, or to take telephone messages).

5. S.T.D. (subscriber trunk dialling). S.T.D. is the Post Office method of charging for telephone calls. A basic rate for a call is charged, but the length of time allowed for the charge varies with the distance of the exchange being called.

Currently, there are lower charges (*i.e.* longer times are allowed) for calls made before 8 a.m. and after 6 p.m., but since the rates are always being altered, it is advisable to check with the local post office for the current rates being charged.

Another feature of S.T.D. is that by dialling the appropriate code (see Dialling Instruction Book) a caller can be connected automatically with any telephone exchange on S.T.D. in the U.K.

A further interesting aspect of S.T.D. is that it is possible, by dialling the appropriate number, to obtain automatically many European countries as well.

6. Telephone etiquette.

(*a*) *Making a call.* Make sure that you know the number you want: do not expect the telephone operator to find out the numbers.

Dial the number carefully, and if your finger slips replace the receiver and start again.

When your caller answers, say who you are and who you want.

If possible, always quote the appropriate extension number required.

(*b*) *Answering the telephone.* Answer the telephone promptly, for it gives the caller a good impression.

Do not carry on with a conversation while the telephone rings; say "Excuse me" and answer the telephone.

Identify yourself and your department, *e.g.* "Brown, accounts department". Do not say "Hello".

Always have a pencil and paper handy (*see* **7** below).

If you offer to ring a caller back, be sure you honour that promise.

Never transfer a call to another extension without first making sure that the other extension can deal with the business concerned.

If you are on a P.M.B.X. and ask the operator to get you a call, do not leave the office without leaving a note of where you can be found.

Do not say "Who are you?" but rather "Who is speaking please?"

(c) *Telephone technique generally.* There is no need to shout on the telephone; talk quietly and distinctly.

Hold the mouthpiece about one inch away from your mouth.

If you have difficulty in being heard, lower the pitch of your voice and speak more slowly.

Emphasise consonants; *e.g.* over the telephone "five" becomes "fife".

Replace the telephone receiver carefully, after a courteous "good-bye".

Remember that courtesy and good manners are essential on the telephone at all times.

If one is cut off during a call, it is normal courtesy for the person who made the call to call back.

NOTE: Remember that, with S.T.D., telephone calls are charged according to their length, so that even a local call if continued for 18 minutes can cost your company six times as much as the normal charge for a three-minute S.T.D. call. So keep your calls short; the rule with S.T.D. is *get on* and *get off*, with no social chatting; keep to business matters.

7. Telephone messages. If you answer the telephone, and the person being called is out of the office, be *tactful* and say that he is not in the office. If he is out for the day, there is no need to say where he has gone or why he is not available; it is of no interest to the caller, and a business executive does not always want callers to know about his movements.

However, ask if you can take a message, and the telephone message form shown in Fig. 20 gives some idea of what should be recorded.

XI. OFFICE COMMUNICATIONS

```
Time ..................                    Date ........................
To: ...........................

                    TELEPHONE MESSAGE

Mr. ............................
of ............................................................................................... telephoned
about..... ..........................................................................
          ...........................................................................
          ...........................................................................

He will call again      ☐           Caller's Telephone No. ..................
Please telephone him    ☐           Extension ..................
Urgent                  ☐           Signed ......................
```

FIG. 20.—*Telephone message form*

It is always advisable when taking down a telephone message to read it back to the caller to check that you have recorded it correctly. If necessary, spell a word out (perhaps the caller's name) and use the analogy alphabet, A for "apples", B for "baker", and so on.

8. Personal calls. A call may be booked as a personal call (*i.e.* you are not connected until the person you want is on the line) on payment of a small extra charge.

If the person called cannot be obtained on the telephone, the exchange operator will leave word at the distant exchange for the wanted person to call as soon as possible. The timing of the call does not start until the telephone connection has been made.

It should be noted, however, that with S.T.D. it is possible to find out quickly whether a particular person is obtainable, which in fact may be cheaper than a personal call.

9. Teleprinter. The teleprinter is a kind of electric typewriter on which messages can be typed and transmitted over telegraph lines to another teleprinter at a distance; the message as it is typed at one end simultaneously appears on the teleprinter at the other end of the line. The same teleprinter can be used to send or receive messages.

Teleprinters are used only internally in a business, connecting a head office with its various works, *e.g.* the head offices of newspapers in Fleet Street with their regional offices. The teleprinter is rented from the Post Office and a rental is charged according to the distance between the teleprinters (big business concerns like Shell Mex and Metal Box Company have a number of them in different parts of the U.K.), but after payment of the rental the machine can be used continuously during the day or night without extra charge.

The teleprinter has a keyboard similar to that on a typewriter, except that it types in capital letters only and depression of the shift keys produces figures and symbols.

Teleprinters are important because they represent the fastest written means of communication between one office and another in different parts of the country. With telephone messages, it is usual business practice to send a letter confirming arrangements made on the telephone, but a teleprinter is the equivalent of a telephone with its speed and the precision obtained with a written letter.

10. Telex. The Telex service is provided by the Post Office and involves the use of a special teleprinter on which the user can send messages to and receive them from any other Telex user either in the U.K. or anywhere else in the world. Where the normal teleprinter is for internal use only, Telex is for external use with other business concerns.

A rental for the use of a Telex machine is paid to the Post Office and in addition a call charge must be paid for every call made. The charges made for messages sent on Telex are rather similar to those for S.T.D., giving a varying length of time according to the distances called.

The Telex service has now over 200,000 subscribers all over the world (15,000 in the U.K.), and it represents a remarkably speedy method of communication which grows in popularity every year.

Since the charges for calls depend on their length, then obviously the greatest value is obtained by employing a fast Telex operator. Since the average operator speed may be only about 40 to 50 words a minute, an automatic transmitter can be used which then sends out messages at 66 words per minute.

As with S.T.D., it is possible to dial any other Telex

subscriber by using his appropriate Telex code number, which is often quoted at the top of a company's letterheading.

11. Staff location. When an important executive is out of his office and is wanted urgently, there must be some means of locating him.

A number of methods can be used for staff location, which is really an aspect of communications:

(*a*) *Paging*, or sending out a personal messenger to locate the executive (the method used in hotels), or by telephoning round the extensions. Both of these would be impossible in a large business concern.

(*b*) *Loudspeaker system*, which is often used in factories, and where the telephone operator is connected through to loudspeakers in the factory or store, to announce that "Mr X" is required.

(*c*) *Light signals*, whereby a system of lighted numbers according to a code, *e.g.* "2" (twice), "4" (once), and "6" (twice), is reproduced in lighted signals in various places in the business so that the person called can see the signalling, check his code and then know if he is the one being called.

(*d*) *Radio call system*, which is probably the best method of all, and is where each V.I.P. is issued with a small portable radio receiver, and where the telephone operator can transmit a call over an individual wavelength allotted to each receiver. The person being called then hears a "bleep, bleep" from the receiver in his pocket, and goes to the telephone to see why he is being called.

This is probably the best system of staff location because it is not noisy (like loudspeakers), it cannot be ignored or not seen (like light signals), it does not require the time taken in searching the building, and it therefore gives the greatest speed in locating the person being called, without bothering any other members of staff.

PROGRESS TEST 11

1. What means of internal communication may be used in an office? **(1)** [*U.L.C.I.*

2. Describe *four* methods of intercommunication by which different sections of an office can communicate with one another. In what kind of office situation could each be used? **(1)** [*E.M.E.U.*

3. (*a*) Why is it important to have a thoroughly reliable person as telephonist in a firm?

(*b*) What rules should be observed in answering the telephone to an outside caller? (**1, 6**) [*Y.C.F.E.*

4. Describe the services provided by the Post Office to enable a businessman to communicate with his customers. (**2, 9, 10**) [*U.L.C.I.*

5. Describe a personal telephone call. (**3**) [*W.J.E.C.*

6. Your office manager is engaging a new telephone operator. What qualities would he look for in the successful applicant? Prepare a list of instructions for her guidance in the correct use of the telephone. (**4**)

[*Y.C.F.E.*

7. Complaints have been received about the telephone manners of some of your junior employees. Outline the steps you would take to remedy the situation, emphasising the points to which you would pay particular attention. (**6**) [*R.S.A.*

8. (*a*) What instructions should be given to telephone users in a firm in order to avoid unnecessary expense when making calls by S.T.D.?

(*b*) Describe the Telex service of the Post Office. (**6, 10**)

[*N.C.T.E.C.*

9. Draft a form for recording incoming telephone messages and enter *one* specimen call. (**7**) [*U.L.C.I.*

10. Mr H. Williams telephones your office to speak to the accountant, Mr J. K. King. Mr King is not available. What action would you take? (**7**) [*Y.C.F.E.*

11. You are employed in the office of Super Stationery Ltd., and at 10.30 a.m. on 3rd June you receive the following telephone call:

"John Brewster here, Benington Ltd. Is Mr James there?" You are the only person in the office, so you ask if you can take a message. Mr Brewster replies:

"Yes please. We're shipping agents and Mr James has an African consignment. Will you tell him that there's some cargo space available on S.S. *Oroma* to Mombasa. It's loading at King George V Dock, London. They're starting on the 7th June, and won't take anything after the 11th. I'd like confirmation before 4.30 this afternoon, so ask Mr James to ring back, please, before then. Would you like to take the number? It's Maxwell 37184. If I'm out, ask for Mr Smith—he'll be able to deal with the job. Thank you, goodbye."

Draw up a suitable telephone message form for general use, and record the essential points of the conversation ready for Mr James' return. (**7**) [*R.S.A.*

12. Write a brief account of the Telex service. (**10**) [*W.J.E.C.*

13. Your switchboard operator complains that she spends much of her time in locating staff to accept incoming telephone calls. Suggest some solutions to this problem. (**11**) [*Y.C.F.E.*

CHAPTER XII

FILING AND RECORDS

1. Filing. This is the basis of all record keeping, and comprises the methods of arranging, indexing and storing records so that they can be located when required.

Often viewed as a routine and boring job, filing is important because the records of a business contain information which may be vital to management decisions and future action. It is important that various records should be kept in such a way that immediate access is possible when required. Secondly, unless records are stored correctly, they can deteriorate, becoming dirty and torn, etc. Thirdly, it is very convenient for management to have records about a certain subject or about a certain action, or even about customers in a certain area, grouped so that a picture can be obtained according to that grouping. Fourthly, good records management ensures that only important papers are kept and the less important ones are thrown away at intervals.

2. Essentials of a good filing system. The word "system" here is very broad in meaning, and as well as the method of classification (*see* **6** below) it can include the equipment, the staffing, and the methods used when referring to records or borrowing from them.

However, in general, the system should satisfy the following requirements:

(*a*) *Compactness*. The system should not take up too much space, particularly floor space.

(*b*) *Accessibility*. The record cabinets, for example, should not be stored at a height of more than six feet.

(*c*) *Simplicity*. The system (particularly its classification) should be simple to understand and simple to operate.

(*d*) *Safety*. The right degree of safety should be ensured for the documents according to their relative importance (*e.g.* by having filing cabinets that are kept locked when not in use, or having really fireproof cabinets).

(*e*) *Economy*. The system should be economical in cost of labour and materials.

(*f*) Records should be capable of being produced with the minimum delay.

(*g*) Cross-references should be provided where necessary (*see* **5** below).

(*h*) *Elasticity*. The system should be capable of being expanded to suit the increased requirements of the business.

(*i*) Records should always be filed up to date, although this may depend on having adequate staffing and on the flow of work.

(*j*) Some system of "out guides" may be advisable (*see* **3** below).

(*k*) The most suitable system of classification should be used (*see* **6** below).

OUT GUIDE							
File	Date	Dept.	Signature	File	Date	Dept.	Signature

Fig. 21.—*Out guide*.

3. Out guides (or tracers). One of the difficulties with filing arises when somebody borrows a file (or even a single letter from a file) and when it is needed the file is found to be missing and its whereabouts unknown.

To overcome this difficulty, it is often advisable to have a system of inserting an "out guide" in the place of the file (or paper) borrowed, which contains information about who has the file, their department and the date borrowed. An example is shown in Fig. 21.

Where many files are borrowed frequently, such a system of using out guides would be inadvisable, but where the files are very important, such as patients' records in a hospital, it might be a matter of life and death if the file cannot be located.

XII. FILING AND RECORDS

4. Follow-up. It often happens in business that it is necessary to check that a reply is received to a particular outgoing letter (perhaps before writing elsewhere), and so there must be some system of follow-up to check that a reply has in fact been received.

The first, and simplest, method is to write a reminder in a diary, dated (say) a week's time after sending a letter, that there is a need to check on the receipt of a reply, and, if there is no reply, perhaps to send a reminder.

Secondly, a special follow-up file can be created which has divisions numbered 1 to 31, corresponding to the days in a month. When a letter is sent out (say) on the 3rd, then a carbon copy of the letter will be placed in the file to be examined (say) one week later, *i.e.* on the 10th. Every day it is the task of the filing clerk to examine the file for that day and to see if replies have in fact been received to the letters which are filed under that day.

Usually, the carbon copies filed are extra copies and are not the ones placed on the permanent files, and if a reply has been received then the third copy can be destroyed. If not, then the absence of a reply must be reported to the writer of the letter.

5. Cross-reference. It often happens that letters might quite reasonably be filed under either one of two alternative headings. For example, a letter about two different contracts might be filed under either of the contracts.

One method of dealing with the situation might be to make a third copy (either an additional carbon or a copy made on the

---

CROSS-REFERENCE

Letter dated :

ABOUT :

SEE :

FIG. 22.—*Cross-reference.*

office photocopier) and place a copy on each file.

An alternative method is to insert a special card or paper in one file which acts as a cross-reference to the carbon copy placed on another file. An example is shown in Fig. 22.

6. Methods of classification. Classification refers to the method of arranging folders or papers in a filing system. Thus letters might be arranged alphabetically according to the names of correspondents, or in accordance with the subject-matter of the correspondence (staffing, insurance, advertising, etc.).

Classification is important because the best method of classification gives the greatest convenience and speed when referring to the filing system and, in addition, causes the least number of filing errors.

The methods of classification are as follows:

(*a*) Alphabetical.
(*b*) Numerical.
(*c*) Geographical.
(*d*) Subject.
(*e*) Chronological.
(*f*) Some combination of classifications (*a*) to (*e*).

These are dealt with in detail in **7–12** below.

7. Alphabetical classification. Documents are filed according to the first letters in the name and then in order of initials or second names.

(*a*) *Advantages:*

  (*i*) Convenience of grouping papers by name of company, etc.
  (*ii*) Direct filing, with no index required.
  (*iii*) Simple and easy to understand.
  (*iv*) Useful provision for miscellaneous papers.

(*b*) *Disadvantages:*

  (*i*) In large systems, it takes longer to find papers.
  (*ii*) Congestion under common names.
  (*iii*) Papers may reasonably be filed under different headings.
  (*iv*) Difficulty of forecasting space requirements for different letters of the alphabet.

(*c*) *Examples.* Filing of correspondence, contracts, staff records.

8. Numerical classification. Each document or folder is given a number and <u>filed in serial number order</u>. A common variant is decimal-numerical (as used in libraries), where each class has ten subdivisions, each of which has ten more subdivisions, and so on.

(*a*) *Advantages:*
  (*i*) Greater accuracy in filing.
  (*ii*) The file number can be used as a reference.
  (*iii*) Unlimited expansion is possible.
  (*iv*) The index is a complete list and can be used for other purposes, *e.g.* as an address index.

(*b*) *Disadvantages:*
  (*i*) More time required in referring to the index.
  (*ii*) Files for miscellaneous papers are not so easy to arrange.
  (*iii*) Cost of the index and space taken by it.
  (*iv*) Transposition of figures causes errors in filing.

(*c*) *Examples.* Filing of sales invoices, contracts (if numbered), committee minutes.

9. Geographical classification. The papers or files are divided according to geographical location. Either part or full geographical classification can be used, *e.g.* London, Provincial and Overseas, for correspondence.

(*a*) *Advantages:*
  (*i*) Convenience of reference where the location is known.
  (*ii*) A measure of direct filing is usual.

(*b*) *Disadvantages:*
  (*i*) Possibility of error where knowledge of geography is weak.
  (*ii*) Geographical location must be known.
  (*iii*) There may be need for an occasional index.

(*c*) *Examples.* Filing of customers' orders in sales area order, correspondence according to town.

10. Subject classification. The documents are arranged in accordance with the subject-matter, instead of with the names of the companies, correspondents, etc.

(*a*) *Advantages:*
  (*i*) Convenience of reference when the subject alone is known.
  (*ii*) Unlimited expansion.

(b) *Disadvantages:*

(i) Difficulty of classification.
(ii) Not very suitable for miscellaneous papers.
(iii) Liberal cross-references may be needed.
(iv) An index may be needed.

(c) *Examples.* Filing of orders according to materials in the buying department, filing of contracts, correspondence, such as legal, insurance, staff, etc.

11. Chronological classification. The documents are filed in order of their date. This system is rarely used absolutely, but it is the usual method of filing papers inside each folder: but *see* "follow-up" in **4** above.

(a) *Advantage.* It is useful if the dates are known when referring to the files.

(b) *Disadvantages:*

(i) It is not always very suitable.
(ii) Incoming letters might become separated from outgoing ones if filed in strict chronological sequence.

(c) *Examples.* Follow-up files as mentioned in **4** above, and when filing purchase invoices ready for payment.

12. A combination of any of classifications 7–11. One such combination might be the alpha-numerical system, as used in a Sales Ledger classification, where the accounts are numbered A1, A2, A3, etc., so that they are in the order of opening them. This is often the most flexible method, and the most popular, since the advantages of several classifications together may be retained.

13. Choosing the system of classification.

(a) What is the most convenient method of reference? (For example, it is inadvisable to file under the invoice number if this is never quoted.)

(b) Size of the system. (Larger systems are nearly always numerical.)

(c) Simplicity in use. (The alphabetical classification is usually thought to be the simplest to understand.)

(d) Ease of expansion. (The numerical classification is usually the easiest to expand.)

(e) Does it minimise the possibility of misfiling? (The

numerical classification is usually most precise.)

(*f*) Does it give the greatest speed of reference? (The numerical classification is not so quick if it means constant reference to an index.)

14. Rules for filing alphabetically. Some general rules for filing alphabetically are as follows:

(*a*) All surnames should be filed in strict alphabetical order, and then in the order of Christian names.

(*b*) If a company has initials only and not Christian names, then it sould be filed in the order of the initials.

(*c*) "The" in front of a name is ignored in filing.

(*d*) Names beginning with prefixes like "Mac" and "Mc" might be placed in front of the bulk of the "M" files, and then in the order of the following names; thus: McIntyre, MacNab, McTaggart, etc.

(*e*) Where firms have numbers incorporated in their names, then they are filed as if the numbers are spelt out; *e.g.* "1960 Cleaners Ltd." would be filed as "Nineteen Sixty Cleaners Ltd."

(*f*) Public authorities are usually filed under the name of the authority; thus "Borough of Bromley" would be filed as "Bromley (Borough of)."

(*g*) Titles in front of names of people are usually ignored; thus "Sir James Cannon" would be filed as "Cannon, James (Sir)."

(*h*) Titles in company names, such as "St" or "Saint", are usually filed as Saint; thus "St John Courtney Salon" would be filed as "Saint John Courtney Salon".

(*i*) Double-barrelled names like "Watts-Owen" are filed as if they are one continuous name.

(*j*) Where a partnership has "and" between the two names, it is also treated as one word; thus "Smith and Jones" is filed as "Smithandjones".

(*k*) When filing hotel names, it is usual to file under the actual name of the hotel; thus "The Hotel Metropole" is filed as "Metropole Hotel (The)".

(*l*) When a company is well known by its initials, such as I.C.I., it can be filed as I.C.I. or under its full name "Imperial Chemical Industries Ltd.", but care must be taken that it is not filed under both, *i.e.* duplicate files.

Arising from this last point, it would be advisable to have a typewritten filing guide which is a list of all files in existence, and to not allow new files to be opened without authority of a senior person.

15. Central filing. Instead of each office maintaining its own filing, central filing is where all (or some) of the business records of different departments are filed in one room together. It means that all papers about the same subjects are filed together on common files in the central filing department. Departments wishing to refer to papers then borrow the files from the central filing department.

Note that it is not always necessary to choose between either central filing or decentralised filing systems, for in many businesses the different offices maintain their own current files while the central filing department keeps out-dated files and becomes the reserve storage.

Even when "central filing" is adopted, however, it would not be suitable when (*a*) the business is widespread geographically; (*b*) confidential documents are filed; or (*c*) documents are the concern of one department only (*e.g.* sales invoices).

(*a*) *Advantages:*

(*i*) Uniformity of filing procedures.
(*ii*) Development of specialist filing staff.
(*iii*) Improved supervision of filing and records.
(*iv*) It fixes responsibility for filing (which is often done by anyone inside a department with time to spare).
(*v*) It ensures that all correspondence about the same subject is filed together (often very convenient).
(*vi*) It eliminates duplication of copies in different departments.
(*vii*) It gives management better control of records.
(*viii*) It helps familiarise staff with the idea that records are the common property of the business.

(*b*) *Disadvantages:*

(*i*) Lack of departmental knowledge by filing staff.
(*ii*) Delay in files being made available.
(*iii*) The larger the filing system, the easier it is to lose individual records.
(*iv*) There is no opportunity for juniors to learn about filing techniques.
(*v*) It may mean extra staff if staff are not released from the departments.

XII. FILING AND RECORDS

16. Indexing. The purpose of an index is to indicate where something can be found (the index finger is the pointing finger). For example, sales invoices might be filed numerically, but so that one can be found without knowing the invoice number a separate alphabetical card index might be maintained which gives the relevant numbers to each customer.

Different forms of index are as follows:

(*a*) Book or ordinary page index, which is simple and cheap (suitable, say, for telephone numbers).

(*b*) Loose or vertical card index (always a live index and in the desired order).

(*c*) Visible card index.

(*d*) Wheel index (or rotary).

(*e*) Strip index.

17. Visible card index. This is where index cards are hinged and filed flat on top of one another in shallow metal trays, overlapping so as to reveal a one-line title to each card (as many as sixty or seventy cards can be seen at a glance when the tray is withdrawn from the cabinet). The trays of cards are housed in metal cabinets and slide in and out as required, and entries can be made on the cards without taking the trays from the cabinet.

(*a*) *Advantages:*

(*i*) Speed of reference.

(*ii*) Use of coloured signals, very useful to indicate action to be taken (*e.g.* for further supplies required on stock records).

(*iii*) Protection from dust and dirt in the metal cabinets.

(*iv*) The cards do not get "dog-eared" and are protected by plastic strips along the lower edges.

(*v*) It is easy to insert new cards or take out old ones; as a consequence, it is always a live index.

(*vi*) Entries can be made on the cards without withdrawing them from the system.

(*b*) *Disadvantages:*

(*i*) The cabinets and cards are relatively expensive.

(*ii*) Speed of reference might be slow when several people are referring to the cards at the same time.

(*iii*) The coloured signals sometimes become loose and fall out.

18. Wheel index (rotary). A modern development in indexing is the wheel or rotary index, whereby the index cards are mounted round a drum. The cards are usually attached by one or two holes punched in the lower edges of the cards, and the cards are easily attached or detached from the drum. Several thousand cards can be accommodated on one drum.

An advanced version of the wheel index is where large-sized wheels are housed in the bodies of specially made desks, and literally millions of cards can be referred to quickly and easily without effort.

19. Strip index. Where reference is required to a one-line title only (*e.g.* names and addresses or telephone numbers) then a strip index is suitable. This consists of the one-line information for each item being typed on narrow strips of thin wood or cardboard, the ends of which are mounted in flanges of a flat metal frame. The frames are hinged and swing from desk or from wall stands.

Again, it gives speed of reference to thousands of items in a series, but only for one-line pieces of information.

20. Filing equipment. The main items of filing equipment found in offices are as follows:

(*a*) *Loose-leaf binders*. These can be of either ring, thong or post variety.

(*b*) *Box files*. These are files which are exactly like a box with a hinged lid, where the papers are held fast by a spring clip inside. These are suitable only for temporary filing or for less important papers such as advice notes, etc.

(*c*) *Concertina files*. These are files which expand (sometimes they are called "expanding files") and which have divisions marked either alphabetically or numerically; a strap goes round an outer cover and keeps the papers enclosed. They are suitable for a small collection of documents such as insurance policies, etc., when the whole file can be placed in the office safe for safe keeping.

(*d*) *Lever-arch files*. In this system the papers have two holes punched down one edge and are filed on the two posts of the arch, the arch being "broken" for the insertion or extraction of papers by the operation of a lever. The lever-arch file is usually accommodated in a cardboard box cover to keep it neat and protect it from dust and dirt.

It is a cheap form of filing and can be used for almost any

office papers (letters, invoices, orders, etc.), but its main disadvantage is that when it becomes over-full, the arch fails to join up correctly and the papers then fall out.

(*e*) *Vertical filing cabinets.* These are metal cabinets usually of four-drawer capacity, where the folders are filed vertically, *i.e.* on edge for ease of reference. These are very common in business, but are apt to be noisy, are relatively expensive to buy, and take up more floor space than some other kinds of equipment (*see* (*g*) below).

(*f*) *Suspended filing.* Pockets are suspended vertically from metal rods which hang from a metal frame or cradle inserted in the filing drawer. With this equipment files are kept neat and upright, and thus it is easy to refer to them and to find a particular folder. The only disadvantages are expense and the extra space taken by the pockets.

(*g*) *Lateral filing.* Suspended files with the end of each file in view are contained in an open framework (*i.e.* not in drawers). Thus lateral filing can be taken to five or six tiers high, saving at least 50 per cent of floor space as compared with vertical filing cabinets. The system is also relatively cheaper.

21. Specific filing equipment.

(*a*) *Plans* can be filed horizontally in shallow drawers of a plan chest, or in a form of vertically suspended files.

(*b*) *Stencils* can also be housed in metal suspended cabinets (rather expensive) or placed in blotting-paper folders and housed in special cardboard folders.

(*c*) *Catalogues*, if in book form, would be on bookshelves, and, if in sheet form, in suspension filing cabinets.

(*d*) *Insurance policies* would be placed perhaps in a concertina file, and kept either in the office safe or at the bank.

22. Microfilming. A common problem with office records is the rate at which they accumulate and the floor space that is consumed by them. To overcome this, first, there should be a planned, regular transfer to reserve storage of inactive records and, secondly, there should be a proper retention programme stating for what periods different records should be kept. A third answer to the problem is microfilming.

This consists of the photographing of office records in

miniature on 16 mm or 35 mm film, the development of the film, and then perhaps the disposal of the records themselves, because it is possible to produce enlarged positives of any microfilm when required. However, the usual method of reference is to have a separate machine called a "viewer" where the microfilm is enlarged and projected on a screen for inspection.

(a) *Advantages:*

(i) Great saving in floor space (as much as 99 per cent).
(ii) Safety (if important, the original documents can be stored in a safe place).
(iii) The problem is overcome of sorting out records to see which are important and which are not.

(b) *Disadvantages:*

(i) Frequent reference via the viewer may be slow and inconvenient.
(ii) Expense of the microfilming (this would have to be compared with the relative cost of floor space).
(iii) The film may be illegible if not processed properly.

23. Wall charts. A number of different wall charts are obtainable for the depicting of current sales, stocks, membership, orders, etc.

(a) Peg-board type with plastic pegs of different colours.
(b) Rack with "T" cards which are housed in slots.
(c) A kind of enlarged visible card index.
(d) Narrow strips of card which are accommodated in slots.
(e) Even ballbearings in vertical slots, to resemble a vertical bar chart.

PROGRESS TEST 12

1. What is filing and why is it important? Discuss the various methods in use for filing correspondence, mentioning the main advantages and disadvantages of each. (**1, 7**) [*W.J.E.C.*

2. (a) Why is the filing of documents indispensable in a firm?

(b) List the following names in alphabetical order for filing or indexing purposes:

XII. FILING AND RECORDS

Urban District of Whitefield	John Smiley
Albert Jones	Bolton Co-operative Society
Sir Samuel Smiles	Professor John Cowan
The Ritz Hotel	Northern Hospital
Albion Rovers F.C.	School of Oriental Studies

(1, 14) [*Y.C.F.E.*

3. (*a*) What are the essential requirements of a good filing system?

(*b*) List the following names in alphabetical order for indexing purposes:

B. White and Co. Ltd.	E. McBride
K. Atkin Ltd.	Hotel Metropol
Dolman and Palmer Ltd.	Dept. of Health and Social Security
Dr W. O'Brien	Dept. of Employment

4. (*a*) Place the following names of individuals, professional bodies and trading organisations in the *order* and *forms* in which you would index them:

L. M. MacIntyre	St John Courtney Salon
The British Plastic Co. Ltd.	E. A. Sanford and Co. Ltd.
1960 Express Services	Denis Donovan
Borough of Bexley	Stephen Watts-Owen
A. M. McBridie	Henry Levene and Co. Ltd.

(*b*) Draw up a typical "out guide" and discuss its importance. **(3, 14)** [*R.S.A.*

5. Describe an efficient system for ensuring that documents requiring action on specific dates are not forgotten but are actually made available on the dates required. **(4)** [*E.M.E.U.*

6. Describe a cross-reference. **(5)** [*W.J.E.C.*

7. Explain the following systems of filing:

(*a*) Alphabetical.
(*b*) Subject.
(*c*) Numerical. **(7, 8, 10)** [*U.L.C.I.*

8. Name four methods of file classification and give examples of the type of work for which they are most suitable. **(7–11)** [*E.M.E.U.*

9. (*a*) Describe a form of suspended filing suitable for general office correspondence.

(*b*) Describe a visible card index. **(7, 17)** [*N.C.T.E.C.*

10. State the advantages of the alpha-numerical system of indexing and filing over the plain alphabetical system. **(14)** [*V.E.I.*

11. Draw up a list of rules for a junior clerk who will be in charge of the filing system in your office while you are on holiday. **(14)**

[*W.J.E.C.*

12. The filing of correspondence in your department is done alphabetically under the name of the correspondent. You are re-

sponsible for this duty which is to be carried out by a junior while you are on holiday. Draw up a list of rules for indexing to enable her to file documents correctly and add any advice you can regarding the handling and sorting of the documents. **(14)** [*R.S.A.*

13. (*a*) Explain the uses and advantages of visible card indexing.
 (*b*) List and prepare an alphabetical index of the following names:

The Fireplace Centre	J. B. McDonald
Dept. of Health and Social Security	Smith and Jones Ltd. Poster Services
A. R. Jackson	Dr. V. W. Bains
J. J. Black and Sons	

(14, 17) [*E.M.E.U.*

14. Discuss the advantages and disadvantages of centralised filing and departmental filing. **(15)** [*Y.C.F.E.*

15. There are six departments in your firm and each keeps its own files in its own way. There is talk of a central filing system, but several departments object. Draw up in two columns a list of arguments for and against a central filing system. **(15)** [*R.S.A.*

16. Name the principal types of index in use. What are the advantages and disadvantages of the visible card index system as compared with the loose card system? **(16, 17)** [*W.J.E.C.*

17. Why is it sometimes necessary to have an indexing system? Describe three modern methods of indexing and indicate the merits of each. **(16, 17, 18)** [*Y.C.F.E.*

18. (*a*) Describe a system of vertical filing suitable for general correspondence.
 (*b*) Describe a rotary card file and give *two* examples of circumstances in which it would be suitable. **(18, 20)** [*N.C.T.E.C.*

19. Describe *two* of the following and indicate their uses in the office:

 (*a*) Rotary filing.
 (*b*) Microfilming.
 (*c*) Visible strip indexing. **(18, 19, 22)** [*R.S.A.*

20. Discuss modern methods of housing files. How would you store (*a*) stencils and (*b*) large-size plans? **(20, 21)** [*Y.C.F.E.*

21. There is a variety of wall charts and similar means of conveying information used in offices. Describe *two* with which you are familiar and outline their advantages. Sketches may be used. **(23)** [*R.S.A.*

CHAPTER XIII

INWARDS AND OUTWARDS MAIL

1. The office mail. Mail in business can for convenience be divided into inwards mail (letters and parcels received) and outwards mail (letters and parcels sent out).

Inwards mail is important because its efficient handling can have a great effect on the working of many departments (*e.g.* orders for the sales department, invoices for the accounts department) and because it may, and usually does, contain important documents as well as cash.

Outwards mail is equally important because unless letters are addressed and stamped correctly, and unless all enclosures are sent with letters it can cause complaints from customers and general inefficiency which can affect the whole of the business (*e.g.* orders for essential materials may go astray).

2. Procedure for inwards mail. While no standard procedure can be laid down, for much will depend on the size of the business and volume of mail received, the following are the main steps involved:

(*a*) Certain clerks (including a senior to supervise) attend about half an hour before the office opens, so that the mail can be distributed by the time other staff arrive.

(*b*) All registered mail is recorded in a separate book and, if not too voluminous, is dealt with by the supervisor in charge.

(*c*) A preliminary sorting can be made into:

(*i*) private, and mail marked "urgent";
(*ii*) sealed envelopes;
(*iii*) unsealed envelopes (less important).

(*d*) All remittances in the post must be checked with remittance advices, monthly statements, etc., which should be ticked (if agreeing with amount sent) and initialled. If a remittance is shown to be incorrect, this must be reported to the supervisor immediately. Other special measures regarding cash are mentioned in 3 below.

(*e*) All letters and other documents should be rubber-stamped with the date of receipt either on the front (care being taken not to obliterate telephone numbers, etc.) or on the reverse.

(*f*) All enclosures must be checked and attached to the letters or other documents enclosed.

(*g*) Letters when opened will be sorted, primarily by the references entered on them; but to save time, if it is uncertain for whom a letter is intended, it should be passed to the supervisor in charge.

(*h*) Some companies distribute letters unopened to various departments, and such a policy saves time in the morning, but many letters are just simply addressed to the company and must be opened before they can be distributed.

(*i*) All empty envelopes must be checked to see that all the contents have been taken out. Sometimes they are opened top and bottom to make sure nothing can remain inside.

(*j*) Mail must be distributed as soon as possible, whenever it is received, although the late afternoon post is sometimes kept until the next day.

(*k*) Some procedure must be established and adhered to where two or more departments need to see the same letter.

(*l*) A properly organised messenger service will then take the sorted mail round to different offices.

NOTE: In some offices dealing with important letters, a record of their receipt may be entered in an inwards mail register, but this has been abandoned in business generally.

3. Dealing with cash, etc.

(*a*) Some businesses rubber-stamp cheques and postal orders with a "crossing" stamp to prevent fraud (*i.e.* to stop their fraudulent negotiation).

(*b*) Cash should be checked by the supervisor.

(*c*) It is advisable to list all remittances (perhaps on an adding machine—or in a special remittance book) and then pass them to the cashier for him to pay into the bank.

(*d*) An internal check should be made, checking the total on the list with the bank paying-in book.

4. Machines and equipment.

(*a*) *Letter-opening machine*, which slices off a narrow strip from the side of the envelope. It is best to make sure that the contents are shaken down to the opposite side first.

(b) *Date-stamp*, perhaps with the name of the department incorporated, and possibly fitted with a time clock for printing the time as well as the date.

(c) *Sorting equipment*, which is of various types. Letters should not be loosely sorted out on top of desks but into wire, wooden or metal trays, pigeon-hole shelving, or even special suspension files (flap sorters save desk space also).

(d) *Photocopying machines* (*see* **5** (*d*) below).

5. Letters for attention of different departments (or persons). This is a common situation in business, and can be dealt with in several different ways:

(a) Writing in pencil at the top of the letter the names of persons or departments who should see the letter.

(b) Sticking on an adhesive label bearing the same information, and a space for the initials of those who have seen the letter.

(c) Use of a special rubber stamp in which there are spaces for the name and initials of people dealing with the letter.

(d) Use of a photocopying machine to make several copies of a letter which are distributed to the different people concerned, the copies being marked with the names of persons or departments who should see the letter.

6. Procedure for outwards mail. As with inwards mail, the procedure will vary from one business to another, but the following steps are usually involved:

(a) Give instructions that letters requiring special attention (registered, foreign mail, etc.) are marked in pencil in the top right-hand corner, drawing attention to the special treatment required.

(b) Institute a regular collection of mail from departments when it is signed. Regular collection of mail during the day helps relieve congestion at the end of the day.

(c) Decide on a deadline at the end of the day, after which letters will not be accepted for despatch (unless there is special permission from an authorised official).

(d) Ensure that all mail is sorted into the different

denominations of postage required (this makes it easier to stamp).

(*e*) Use folding and sealing machines when large quantities of mail are to be posted.

(*f*) To avoid letters being sent in the wrong envelopes, window envelopes should be used wherever possible.

(*g*) Check all "enclosures" on letters to see that the appropriate number of enclosures are actually attached.

(*h*) Decide on the method of stamping (*see* **8** below).

(*i*) If a franking machine is used, ensure that it is returned to the office safe each night.

(*j*) Enter outgoing letters in the post book (*see* **7** below).

(*k*) Instruct the office staff that the office post must not be used for private mail.

(*l*) All Post Office receipts for registered and recorded delivery letters should be gummed into a special book provided.

(*m*) Arrange for the post to be taken to the post box or post office before the last collection.

POST BOOK					
Date	Amount	Date	Name	Address	Amount

Fig. 23.—*Columns of a post book.*

7. The post book. As mentioned above, it is usual for all outgoing mail to be entered in a post book (*see* Fig. 23). It is organised in a similar way to the petty cash book, with the amount of stamps received entered on the left-hand side (*Dr.*) and the letters stamped entered on the right-hand side (*Cr.*). It is often kept on the imprest system (*see* VIII, **4**).

It is not usual to enter full names and addresses from all letters sent out, as name and town are deemed sufficient; in fact if 43 invoices are sent out they are usually entered as "43 Invoices @ ..."

The purpose of keeping a post book is:

(*a*) to have a record of the amount of postage expended;

(*b*) to be able to check on the stock of stamps in hand (*i.e.* if a franking machine is not used); and

(*c*) to have a record for reference purposes of the sending of a letter.

8. Stamping and posting. There are four main methods of stamping:

(*a*) By the purchase of sheets of adhesive stamps from a post office. They should be kept in special folders for each denomination and detached as they are used (care must be taken that loose stamps are not lost).

(*b*) Use of a stamp-emitting or stamp-affixing machine, which automatically records the number of each denomination used. It is necessary to obtain the stamps in rolls from a post office, and to use a different machine for each denomination required.

(*c*) Use of a franking machine (*see* **9** below).

(*d*) By pre-payment at a post office. Provided the total value of stamps is at least 50p, and the number of letters at least 60, the Post Office will frank letters on payment by cheque of the postage incurred.

9. Franking machines. A postal franking machine is a machine purchased privately from the manufacturers, who first have to obtain a licence in the buyer's name from the Post Office.

A lever is set on the machine for the rate of postage desired (it is important to check the setting before use), and on operation the machine prints on the envelope a reproduction of a postage stamp and the date cancellation mark.

Before the machine can be used, advance payment has to be made at the local post office for the value of stamps expected to be used (in say a month), when a meter is set on the machine for that amount. Every day, the franked mail has to be taken to the local post office with a completed docket supplied by the post office for the post franked on the letters. Entry of the meter readings has to be recorded in a special record book.

When the amount prepaid has been used up, the machine locks and has to be taken back to the post office with another cheque for future franking.

The machines record on a dial the amount of postage used, and on bigger machines another dial shows the amount of postage unused as well.

(a) *Advantages:*
  (i) Great *speed* is obtained (it is possible to frank as many as 15,000 letters an hour on an automatic electric machine).
  (ii) *Safety:* it eliminates the use of loose stamps.
  (iii) *Accounting control:* the dials on the machine provide a record of postage expenditure.
  (iv) *Convenience:* the manufacturers of the machines claim that it eliminates the need for keeping a post book.
  (v) *Despatch of mail:* because the letters are already franked, they are not held up for postal franking at the post office.

(b) *Disadvantages:*
  (i) Postage may be wasted by accidentally franking wrong amounts (although refunds can be obtained from the Post Office).
  (ii) Letters have to be taken to the Post Office, instead of merely to the local post box.
  (iii) It may be argued that it does not save the keeping of a post book, since the machine does not record what was sent out.
  (iv) Even with a franking machine, it may still be necessary to have loose stamps in the office for use on receipts, and for urgent letters posted after the Post Office is closed.

10. Machines and equipment.

(a) *Post Office Guide*.
(b) Letter and parcel scales.
(c) Folding machines (fitted with rollers which automatically put a fold in a sheet of paper at the desired position).
(d) Letter-sealing machine.
(e) Stamp folder, stamp-emitting machine or postal franker.
(f) Brown paper, corrugated carboard (for parcels), adhesive tape and string.
(g) Stapling machine and supplies of clips, pins, etc.

11. Business Reply system. This Post Office service enables a business to send out unstamped reply cards or leaflets which the recipients can mail back to the original sender without having to pay postage. It is greatly used for soliciting business, guarantee cards, etc. The business then makes itself responsible for the postal charges on all replies received. Arrangements for printing the cards and the cost of doing so must also be borne by the business.

Post Office requirements are as follows:

(*a*) A licence must first be obtained from the local Head Postmaster (plus an annual licence fee).

(*b*) A deposit must be paid in advance sufficient to cover charges for a reasonable period.

(*c*) The cards, envelopes, etc., must conform to a pattern laid down by the Post Office; particularly, they must have two wide black vertical lines near the right-hand edge.

(*d*) The cards or leaflets returned by the recipients are then delivered to the licensee through the post in the normal way: a charge of 1p for each one in addition to normal postage is then due. Against this, the deposit previously paid is offset.

12. Sending money through the post. There are five main methods:

(*a*) *By cheque*. This is perhaps the most convenient method and the one that gives the greatest security. Note the alternatives of traders' credit and credit transfer.

(*b*) *By postal order*. This is suitable for small amounts and cases where the recipient may not have a bank account.

(*c*) *By T.M.O.* (*telegraphic money order*). This order is similar to a money order, except that it is sent with greater speed.

(*d*) *By sending notes and coins in a registered envelope*. The envelope must be of the special strong type supplied by the Post Office or similar to it. This method is suitable only for the payment of very small amounts.

13. Urgent letters. It is useful in business to know the different methods of sending letters quickly; the following alternatives are available:

(*a*) *Full express service*. A charge is made of so much per mile according to the distance sent. This is the most expensive method but the one most suitable for short distances.

(*b*) *Special delivery* (also known as "express"). The Post Office arranges for the letter to be specially delivered from the Post Ofice in the area of the addressee, *i.e.* before the normal delivery service.

(c) *Sunday delivery*. In some large towns, letters may be handed in on Saturday for a special Sunday delivery, although this is now a restricted service which is available only at certain main post offices.

(d) *Railway letter*. By arrangement with the Post Office, letters can be handed in at railway stations and will be sent by the next train to the station at the destination, either (i) to be called for or (ii) to be put in the post locally. Envelopes must be marked accordingly.

(e) *Railex*. The Post Office will accept a letter, take it to the nearest railway station and send it by the next train. From here on it is dealt with as is a railway letter.

(f) *Late posting*. For a small extra charge, postal packets can be posted at travelling post offices (*i.e.* sorting carriages on mail trains) up to five minutes before the departure of the train.

NOTE: Rates of postage have purposely been omitted because of changes in rates from time to time; for these reference should be made to the current edition of the *Post Office Guide*.

14. Registered letters and recorded delivery.

(a) *Registered letters*. Any letter or parcel can be registered at the post office. A small fee is charged in addition to normal postage, and the letter, etc., must be fastened with sealing wax and marked with a blue pencil in the centre horizontally and vertically.

The value of sending by registered post is that the sender is given a certificate of posting, that the Post Office will pay compensation if the letter is lost (up to £150 for the lowest registration fee) and that a receipt is obtained when the letter or parcel is delivered.

(b) *Recorded delivery*. This is a cheaper version of registration (about one quarter of the cost) and gives compensation only up to £2. It is expressly stated that it must not be used for money, jewellery, etc., and it cannot be used for parcels. Recorded delivery thus gives greater security than an ordinary letter and some measure of compensation, as well as providing a certificate of posting (*i.e.* proof that the letter has been posted).

Recorded delivery is very useful for the sending of important documents such as contracts, insurance policies, etc., and is cheaper than sending by registered post.

XIII. INWARDS AND OUTWARDS MAIL

15. Overseas post. Generally speaking letters to countries in the Commonwealth can be sent at the normal inland postage rates, while letters to foreign countries are charged at more than double the rate for merely one ounce. It is important to check with the *Post Office Guide* for the correct rate of postage, and to weigh each letter or parcel very carefully.

(*a*) *Air letters* are those obtainable from the Post Office, which are low priced and form a letter and envelope combined (on thin blue paper).

(*b*) *Airway letters* are those which can be posted at certain air terminals (by arrangement with British Airways) for delivery by the next aeroplane to any country in Europe.

(*c*) *International reply coupons* are exchangeable at post offices abroad for postage stamps and thus enable the sender of a letter to a place abroad to prepay a reply. There are two kinds (at different prices), a Commonwealth reply coupon and an international reply coupon.

16. Window envelopes. These can be used as (*a*) a method of saving in typing or writing addresses on envelopes and (*b*) a precaution against letters being placed in the wrong envelopes and sent to wrong addresses.

However, when these letters are used, it is advisable if the stationery to be used with them is made to a regulation size to suit the envelope, that there are box "corners" printed for the correct positioning of the address, and that there are also small fold marks down one edge of the stationery to give correct folding, again so that the address shows through the window.

There are the "cut-outs" and the "crystal window" varieties, and, considering the advantages, it is surprising that business has not used window envelopes to a greater extent. Although they are more expensive than ordinary envelopes, the advantages gained may be said to outweigh the additional expense involved.

17. Cash on delivery (c.o.d.). Under this service, an amount of money can be collected for the sender by the Post Office before it delivers a parcel.

General regulations about the c.o.d. service are as follows:

(*a*) The amount to be collected must not exceed £50.

(*b*) The sender must write on each parcel or packet:

(i) his name and address;
(ii) the name and address of the addressee;
(iii) the amount of money to be collected (the Post Office calls this the "trade charge").

(c) The sender must complete a trade charge form and affix in the space provided stamps to the value of the c.o.d. fee (additional to normal postage).

(d) A certificate of posting will be given.

(e) When the Post Office delivers the parcel (or letter) and collects the money required, it will send a crossed order for that amount to the sender.

(f) Maximum compensation for an unregistered c.o.d. parcel is £5.

PROGRESS TEST 13

1. There is some concern in your company because letters appear to be going astray. You are asked to devise a system for handling the incoming mail that will ensure the maximum security, especially for remittances. Set out in some detail your plan. (2, 3) [R.S.A.

2. How should the receipt of incoming mail be organised to ensure its prompt and proper handling and distribution within the firm? (2) [Y.C.F.E.

3. Describe the procedure that would be adopted by a large organisation, with a central mailing room, for the speedy opening, sorting and distributing of the morning post. Mention any special security precautions that might be introduced. (2, 3) [E.M.E.U.

4. Describe the action which has to be taken to ensure that the post which arrives in the morning is opened and distributed quickly and safely. (2) [N.C.T.E.C.

5. Give *four* important rules to observe when opening the morning mail. (2) [W.J.E.C.

6. Describe the opening, sorting and distribution of the inward mail of an office with several departments. How should (a) remittances and (b) urgent letters requiring the attention of more than one department be dealt with? (2, 3, 5) [E.M.E.U.

7. Describe a procedure that could be introduced by a large organisation for dealing with its outward mail. (6) [E.M.E.U.

8. What arrangements would you make for dealing efficiently with a large and varied outward mail? Mention the equipment you would use to speed up the work and also what steps you would take to ensure that enclosures are not omitted. (6, 10) [W.J.E.C.

9. As the petty cashier of your firm you are responsible for buying postage stamps. How would you satisfy the chief cashier that the

money spent had actually been used on the purchase of stamps? Illustrate your answer by showing two entries in a specimen ruling of a postage book. (**7**) [*E.M.E.U.*

10. State briefly the purpose of the post book and name the department in which it is likely to be used. (**7**) [*R.S.A.*

11. (*a*) Why is it desirable to use a post book?

(*b*) Draft a page of ruling for a post book.

(*c*) Make at least six entries of three different types. (**7**) [*U.L.C.I.*

12. Describe the system whereby the cash for postage stamps is provided by the cashier on the imprest system. (**7**) [*U.E.I.*

13. Write a report for your office manager setting out the benefits to be derived by the installation of a franking machine to replace the present system of dealing with the outgoing mail. (**9**) [*U.E.I.*

14. Describe any *four* of the following machines: (*a*) postal franker, (*b*) letter folder, (*c*) envelope sealer, (*d*) collator, (*e*) adding-listing machine, (*f*) cash register. (**9, 10**) [*N.C.T.E.C.*

15. Outline the necessary action which has to be taken in the post department when dealing with the following:

(*a*) Post Office docket for your franking machine.

(*b*) Magazines for circulation within the firm.

(*c*) Printed papers and samples posted in bulk.

(*d*) Parcels for despatch abroad. (**9, 15**) [*R.S.A.*

16. Give a brief description of some of the equipment that may be employed in handling large quantities of outgoing mail. (**10**)

[*Y.C.F.E.*

17. Write briefly on each of the following Post Office services:

(*a*) Business reply service.

(*b*) Telex service.

(*c*) International reply coupons. (**11, 15**) [*R.S.A.*

18. Discuss the following services offered by the Post Office:

(*a*) Business reply.

(*b*) Railex.

(*c*) Recorded delivery.

(*d*) c.o.d. (**11, 13, 14, 17**) [*E.M.E.U.*

19. Explain the terms (*a*) express delivery and (*b*) Telex. (**12**)

[*Y.C.F.E.*

20. It is 2.30 in the afternoon and you have to get in touch with an applicant for an important post in your organisation to ask him to atttend for interview the following morning at 10.30. State what Post Office services are available to you and whether you could make sure of getting a reply from the applicant if he lives about 40 miles away. (**13**) [*R.S.A.*

21. What is recorded delivery? How is it operated? Are there any restrictions on articles which may be despatched by this method? (**14**)

[*Y.C.F.E.*

22. (*a*) What considerations would influence your choice in deciding whether to use the Post Office's recorded delivery or registered mail service?

(*b*) What special regulations have to be complied with when sending items by the above methods? (**14**) [*E.M.E.U.*

23. What are window envelopes? Give examples of the type of correspondence usually sent in them. State their advantages over ordinary envelopes and suggest any serious disadvantages. (**16**)

[*U.L.C.I.*

CHAPTER XIV

TYPING AND TYPING POOLS

1. Typewriters. A typewriter is a simple, basic office machine, and it is used to produce business letters and documents so that they are presented in a better style and are more readable than they would be if hand-written.

Typewriters are used not only to type letters and reports but also for the preparation of masters for duplicating, for the preparation of index cards, and for the completion of official forms.

As well as the standard office typewriter, business uses the following modifications.:

(*a*) *Noiseless typewriters*. On these machines the throw of the type-bars is checked before hitting the platen (the rubber-covered roller which holds the paper). This typewriter makes less noise than a standard machine but does not make so many carbon copies and is not liked a great deal by typists because of the unusual touch.

(*b*) *Electric typewriters*. Here the type-bars are actuated by an electric motor. These machines are faster, give an even impression and produce as many as twenty carbon copies. But, unless typists are trained on them, they find the touch very different from a manually operated machine.

(*c*) *Automatic typewriters*. These are a kind of electric typewriter operated automatically by the holes in punched paper tape (or magnetic spots on magnetic tape). Normally, a standard letter is composed and put into punched-tape form, and when this is fed into an electric typewriter the letter is typed at 150 words per minute. Automatic typewriters are of great use when it is wished to send an identical letter to many people but at the same time to make each letter look as if it has been typed individually (*e.g.* credit letters asking customers for money).

(*d*) *Variable type machines*. On these machines different sizes and styles of type can be obtained very easily. This is an expensive kind of electric typewriter used mainly for the preparation of masters for subsequent printing by offset lithography (see XV, **4**).

2. Typing pool (or central typing department). Instead of having typists working in separate offices, a common practice in business is to place them (or most of them) in one large room where they work together and share the work among them. Usually a supervisor is in charge, and either the typists attend different offices to take down letters in shorthand (and return to the pool to type them out) or they use dictating machines (see **4** below) and, with a central dictating system, have no need to leave the typing department at all, because recordings are made in their room, where the transcriptions are then typed.

(a) *Advantages:*
  (i) Makes the most economical use of typists.
  (ii) More even distribution of work.
  (iii) Minimises difficulties due to absence of typists (sickness and holidays).
  (iv) Better training can be provided for juniors.
  (v) Junior duties (*e.g.* answering the telephone) can be delegated to juniors.
  (vi) Working conditions appropriate to typists can be provided.
  (vii) The noise of typing is confined to one room.
  (viii) Improved supervision of typists.
  (ix) Typists have opportunity for wider experience.

(b) *Disadvantages:*
  (i) Lack of personal contact of typists with executives.
  (ii) Not suitable where private secretaries are employed.
  (iii) It may encourage gossiping.
  (iv) It may not suffice where specialised work is involved.
  (v) Lack of continuity of interest on the part of typists.
  (vi) Delays caused by calling typists from the pool.
  (vii) If not already in being, a messenger service will be required to take finished letters back to departments.

3. Private secretaries. Despite the trend towards the establishment of central typing pools, many business managers still like to retain their private secretaries. They are shorthand typists who are given many extra duties (taking minutes of meetings, making arrangements for travel and so on) and who often occupy very senior positions. In fact, they are often referred to as "P.A.s" (personal assistants) and may act as deputies to the executives when they are away from the office.

4. Dictating machines. These are electronic machines which record speech on various recording media, so that a typist can play back the recording and transcribe it on her typewriter.

There are two main types of dictating machine available: (*a*) the magnetic, which records on tape, disc, etc., and which can be used over and over again, and (*b*) the inscribed, where a track is cut in the recording media rather like a gramophone record, but which cannot be used again.

(*a*) *Advantages:*
  (*i*) Reduces the number of typists required (because they do not spend time in writing shorthand, only in typing).
  (*ii*) Convenience to the dictator, who can record at any time and at any speed.
  (*iii*) The machine can be used for recording telephone conversations, interviews, etc.
  (*iv*) In typing pools it enables dictation to be shared among the typists (overcoming the difficulty of reading other people's shorthand).
  (*v*) Assists in supervision: typists have of necessity to wear hearing devices on their ears, which makes it difficult to gossip.

(*b*) *Disadvantages:*
  (*i*) Typists usually dislike dictating machines (they lose their shorthand skill).
  (*ii*) It requires training of dictators more than of typists.
  (*iii*) Typists are not in close contact with the executives and may lose some of the interest in the job.
  (*iv*) With magnetic recordings, there is always the risk of accidental erasure of dictation.

PROGRESS TEST 14

1. Describe the uses of typewriters in general office work. What advantages have electric typewriters over standard typewriters? (**1**)
[*N.C.T.E.C.*

2. Name and briefly describe four different kinds of typewriter, other than a standard machine, used in offices today. (**1**) [*U.L.C.I.*

3. Describe the functions of *two* machines which can be used in dealing with correspondence and office papers. (**1, 4**) [*U.L.C.I.*

4. What is a typing pool? What are its advantages and disadvantages? (**2**) [*Y.C.F.E.*

CHAPTER XV

DUPLICATING AND PHOTOCOPYING

1. Duplicating. Office duplicating is a process common to every office, and it consists of the preparation of a *master* copy from which a number of other copies can be obtained on what is usually called *copy paper*.

There are three main processes (which are discussed in detail below):

(*a*) Stencil duplicating (*see* **2**).
(*b*) Spirit duplicating (*see* **3**).
(*c*) Offset lithography (*see* **4**).

2. Stencil duplicating. This is where the master copy is a thin sheet of paper covered with a plastic coating through which ink will not pass. The stencil is usually prepared (or cut) on a typewriter and placed on the outside of an inked drum on the machine. As the machine is operated, ink is forced through the cuts in the stencil, providing the image required on absorbent copy paper. The paper must be absorbent, or otherwise the image would smudge. As many as 1,000 copies and more can be obtained from a single stencil, which can be stored and used again.

(*a*) *Advantages:*

(*i*) Ease of altering the stencil (by use of correcting fluid).
(*ii*) Length of run (*i.e.* number of copies) obtainable from each stencil.
(*iii*) Good-quality reproduction.
(*iv*) Photographic reproduction with electronic stencils.
(*v*) Stencils can be stored and used again.
(*vi*) Cheapness of copy paper.

(*b*) *Disadvantages:*

(*i*) Difficulty of registration where two or more colours are required (*i.e.* to make them coincide).
(*ii*) Separate runs required for two or more colours.
(*iii*) The absorbent nature of the copy paper.
(*iv*) Cost of stencils if only a few copies are required.

The stencil method is suitable for any office job where several hundred or even thousands of copies are required, and where good-quality reproduction is also wanted. In particular it is useful for reproducing minutes of meetings, sales literature, price lists and special circular letters to customers or shareholders.

3. Spirit duplicating. With this process, the master copy is a piece of art paper (glossy on one side) prepared by typing or writing on it while it is backed with a piece of special hectographic carbon paper. This creates a reverse image in carbon on the back of the master copy. When the master is placed round a drum on the machine and the machine is operated, the copy paper is dampened with spirit (methylated) so that some of the carbon is dissolved, leaving a positive image on the copy paper.

About 100 to 200 copies can be obtained from each master copy before it is exhausted.

As many as seven colours can be obtained from the master simultaneously, by the consecutive use of different-coloured carbons. Good-quality smooth-surfaced paper is best for use as copy paper.

(*a*) *Advantages:*
   (*i*) Cheapness of both carbon and master paper.
   (*ii*) Ease of preparing the master copy (*e.g.* it can be written with a ball-pen).
   (*iii*) It is the only method by which many colours can be duplicated *simultaneously*.
   (*iv*) Simplicity of preparation.
   (*v*) Good-quality paper used for copies.

(*b*) *Disadvantages:*
   (*i*) The image becomes progressively weaker as the carbon deposit is used up.
   (*ii*) Difficulty of altering the master copy if mistakes are made.
   (*iii*) Limited number of copies from each master.
   (*iv*) Quality of reproduction is not as good as that from a stencil.

4. Offset lithography. This is really a printing process; the basic principle is that it relies on the antipathy (*i.e.* common rejection of each other) of grease and water. The master copy is usually a metal plate photographically prepared. It is placed on the machine where it comes in contact with greasy ink and water, and the positive image on the plate is offset (or transferred) to a rubber-covered roller, giving a negative image. When paper is fed between this roller and an impression roller, it receives the final positive image.

Almost any paper can be used for the copy paper, and separate runs have to be made for different colours.

The reason why this machine is included in office duplicating is because paper masters can be prepared on a typewriter using a special greasy inked ribbon, from which a thousand or more copies can be obtained. This gives a relatively cheap form of duplicating. Paper plates can also be photographically prepared on some photocopying machines.

As it is really a printing process and costs several hundred pounds, an offset lithography machine would not be purchased unless office printing was intended, but once installed it provides a cheap form of duplicating.

(*a*) *Advantages:*

  (*i*) It is a cheap form of printing.
  (*ii*) The quality of reproduction is best of all.
  (*iii*) Any paper can be used.
  (*iv*) It reproduces photographically (*i.e.* not merely typewritten matter).
  (*v*) Length of run (50,000 or more can be obtained from a metal plate).
  (*vi*) Convenience to the management (particularly when a printed form is suddenly found to be out of stock).

(*b*) *Disadvantages:*

  (*i*) Separate runs required for different colours.
  (*ii*) A trained operator is required—more so than for stencil or spirit duplicating.
  (*iii*) It is more expensive in capital outlay.
  (*iv*) It requires a great deal of office space for chemicals, plate and paper storage, etc.

Offset lithography can be used for any office job where a printed appearance is required, and where long runs of many thousands may be wanted. It is particularly useful for printing sales leaflets, staff magazines, internal office forms and catalogues (even with photographs of products, etc.).

5. Storage of master copies.

(*a*) *Spirit masters* do not store very well because the carbon is apt to become smudged; furthermore they are so cheap that it is hardly worth keeping them.

(*b*) *Stencil masters* on the other hand should be housed in special blotting paper folders, and either kept in indexed folders or housed in suspended files in metal filing cabinets.

(*c*) Similarly *offset litho masters* are best kept in suspended filing cabinets which are specially made for this purpose.

6. Photocopying. While office duplicating is used to provide many copies from a master copy, photocopying is used to provide a single copy or a few copies only of an *original*, *i.e.* something not specially prepared but rather like a cutting from a newspaper.

There are *four* main methods of photocopying, discussed in detail below:

(*a*) Transfer diffusion (*see* **7**).
(*b*) Dyeline (*see* **8**).
(*c*) Thermographic (*see* **9**).
(*d*) Electrostatic (*see* **10**).

7. Transfer diffusion. This is perhaps the most popular type of machine in use and it is the cheapest one to buy. Usually the original is fed into the machine sandwiched between a piece of negative and a piece of positive paper. After exposure to light the original is removed. The negative and positive sheets go through a combined developer and fixer, and finally they are peeled apart, when the image will have been transferred from the negative to the positive paper.

(*a*) *Advantages*:
  (*i*) Very good-quality reproduction.
  (*ii*) Any document in colour can be copied.
  (*iii*) It can be used to create offset litho plates.
  (*iv*) Translucent masters can be created for further copy by dyeline.

(*b*) *Disadvantages*:
  (*i*) It uses wet chemicals, which need constant renewing.
  (*ii*) Negatives are re-usable, but not very easily.
  (*iii*) It is sensitive to direct daylight.

8. Dyeline. The originals in this process need to be on transparent or translucent paper. The method consists of placing the original in contact with special dyeline paper and exposing it to light (no negative is employed); the light bleaches the paper white except where the image occurs. The image is then fixed by chemical fumes or wet chemicals.

(a) *Advantages:*

(i) It is the cheapest method of photocopying.
(ii) It can be used in ordinary daylight.
(iii) It is used a great deal in office systems.
(iv) The originals can be stored and used again.

(b) *Disadvantages:*

(i) Originals need to be translucent or transparent and single-sided only.
(ii) Not such good-quality reproduction as transfer diffusion.

9. Thermographic. Here the equipment contains an infrared lamp which emits heat. The original is fed into the machine along with a piece of special heat-sensitive paper. A copy is then automatically produced without wet chemicals at all, and in a matter of seconds.

The ink on the original needs to have a carbon content or it will not copy; thus ordinary ball-pen ink does not reproduce, although special "reproduction" ball-pens can be obtained which will copy.

(a) *Advantages:*

(i) The fastest method of all (four seconds).
(ii) Completely dry; no wet chemicals are used.
(iii) Spirit duplicating masters can be made photographically on it.
(iv) Very simple to operate.

(b) *Disadvantages:*

(i) Heat-sensitive paper does not give a very good-quality image.
(ii) It copies only originals of which the ink has a carbon content.
(iii) Some colours (red, green, etc.) will not copy at all.

NOTE: A new version of this method, known as "Dual Spectrum", which will copy ball-pen ink and colours is now on the market, but its running costs are much more expensive.

10. Electrostatic. On an electrostatic machine, the image from the original is projected on to a selenium-coated plate charged with electricity. Powdered ink, also charged with electricity, is showered over the plate, and when ordinary paper is placed in contact with the plate the ink adheres to it. The ink is then fused on the paper by the application of heat.

(a) *Advantages:*

(i) No wet chemicals are involved.
(ii) It uses ordinary paper.
(iii) Good-quality reproduction.
(iv) An unlimited number of copies of the original are obtainable.

(b) *Disadvantages:*

(i) It is suitable only for a large volume of work, because of the relatively high cost of the machine.
(ii) Sometimes repeated maintenance is required.
(iii) It will not copy all colours equally well.
(iv) With a large volume of work, the selenium drum has to be replaced at intervals, and the quality of the image fades.

PROGRESS TEST 15

1. Your sales manager is circularising about 200 customers informing them of a new product. You have at your disposal a spirit duplicating machine, a stencil duplicating machine and an automatic typewriter. Discuss the suitability of each for this application. (**2, 3**) [*Y.C.F.E.*

2. Describe briefly (*a*) the spirit method and (*b*) the stencil method of duplicating and the relative advantages and disadvantages of each method. (**2, 3**) [*E.M.E.U.*

3. What method of reproduction would you advise for each of the following jobs? Explain the reasons for your choice in each case.

(*a*) A congratulatory message from the chairman of a large group of retail stores to his four most outstanding branch managers.

(*b*) One thousand copies of a price-list amendment.

(*c*) Twenty thousand copies of a two-colour handbill, incorporating a photograph.

(*d*) Fifty copies of an agenda for the works' first-aid group committee meeting. (**2, 3, 4**) [*E.M.E.U.*

4. Your employer wishes to install a duplicating machine in the office. Write a short report for him on the various methods of duplication which are available, indicating the type of work for which each method is most suitable. (**2, 3, 4**) [*W.J.E.C.*

5. State, with reasons, the methods you recommend for preparing the following:

(*a*) Twelve copies of a technical report, which includes diagrams, prepared by your works manager.

(b) One copy of each of six invoices requested by your auditor.

(c) Thirty copies of your company's annual accounts for distribution among shareholders.

(d) 1,200 copies of a quarterly house magazine. (**2, 3, 4, 7**)
[*Y.C.F.E.*

6. Compare offset litho and stencil duplicating as means of catering for the duplicating needs of an office. (**2, 4**) [*N.C.T.E.C.*

7. What instructions should be given to a newly appointed junior on the preparation, running off and storage of stencils? (**2, 5**) [*E.M.E.U.*

8. Describe in non-technical terms a system of stencil duplication and a method of photocopying with which you are familiar. (**2, 7**)
[*U.L.C.I.*

9. A new spirit duplicator is to be installed in your office. What supplies will be necessary for its use? Briefly explain the purpose of these and their use. (**3**) [*Y.C.F.E.*

10. (a) Say what you know about offset lithography.

(b) What advantages and disadvantages can be claimed for this method of printing? (**4**) [*E.M.E.U.*

11. There are 3,024 customers' names in your firm's mailing list. Your superior gives you an advertising circular letter and instructs you to send a copy to each customer. Describe stage by stage the procedure that you would follow in dealing with this matter, indicating the machines you would use to assist you. (**4**) [*U.E.I.*

12. Describe two of the following methods of reprography, outlining the advantages and disadvantages, and comment on the type of copy produced by each method:

(a) Dyeline equipment.
(b) Direct transfer photocopying.
(c) Offset lithography. (**4, 7, 8**) [*R.S.A.*

CHAPTER XVI

BOOKS OF REFERENCE

1. Reference in the office. There is often a need in offices to refer to various facts, and an office worker should be aware of the various books of reference that can be consulted.

However, it must not be imagined that all information can be found in books (they are often out of date for one thing), and references can be made either on the telephone (if urgent) or by letter to any of the following bodies:

(*a*) Local chambers of commerce (for local information about business affairs).

(*b*) Local chambers of trade (for information about retail business afairs).

(*c*) Various government departments (*e.g.* Department of Trade, Department of Employment).

(*d*) Trade associations (according to the industry concerned).

(*e*) Local authorities (for information about parking facilities, etc.).

2. Books of reference. Books of reference can be broadly classified into those concerned with travel, Post Office facilities, and so on, but there are a number of general books of reference which provide all manner of varied information.

In addition, it is possible to ascertain the same information in different books; thus mileage to different places in the U.K. can be sought in the *A.A. Handbook* and the *A.B.C. Railway Guide*, as well as in a good gazetteer.

When drawing up a set of reference books for use in an office, it would be advisable to include at least one of each of the categories set out below.

3. Names and addresses and trades.
(*a*) *Telephone directories.* All large cities and country areas have their own telephone directories giving names, addresses and telephone numbers of subscribers.

Of particular interest are the classified telephone directory and the *Yellow Pages* directory, which have all businesses in an area arranged alphabetically under the trade or profession. They are therefore ideal for obtaining names of manufacturers or traders in special materials.

(*b*) *Street directories*. These are published by the Post Office and give the names of streets and the names of occupiers of houses, offices, shops, etc., identified by their house number. These are arranged alphabetically under street names; trades and professions are also listed.

4. Post Office Guide. This is published annually by the Post Office, and gives full details of all postal, telephone, telegram, overseas mail and other services provided by the Post Office. It is a necessity for every office, and must be kept up to date because changes in postage, etc., are always being made. When one is purchasing a *Post Office Guide*, a request can be made to the local postmaster to send free of charge monthly supplements on the current changes in the regulations.

5. English reference books. In every office, there arise problems of spelling, phrasing, sentence construction, and so on, and for writing letters synonyms are often useful to know. To this end, there should be provided:

(*a*) a good English dictionary;
(*b*) *The Complete Plain Words*, by Sir Ernest Gowers (a workaday book on English published by H.M.S.O.);
(*c*) *Roget's Thesaurus of English Words and Phrases*.

6. Travel information.

(*a*) For *rail* travel, the *A.B.C. Railway Guide* gives times of train departures and arrivals and details of stations *en route*. The names of stations are arranged in alphabetical order, and the *Guide* gives some details of fares.

(*b*) For *road* travel, the A.A. or the R.A.C. *Handbook* gives information about hotels at different places in the U.K., brief details about towns (particularly their early closing days) and motor repair garages. Both the motoring bodies will provide members with itineraries for journeys between any points in the U.K.

(*c*) For *sea* travel there is an *A.B.C. Shipping Guide*, and

Lloyd's List also gives details of ship movements, which are also quoted in some national newspapers.

7. Forms of address. It often happens in business that persons of rank have to be written to, and it is therefore necessary to know how they should be addressed, in what order their degrees should be placed, and so on.

To help in this connection the following would be useful:

(*a*) *Black's Titles and Forms of Address.*

(*b*) *Debrett's Peerage and Titles of Courtesy.*

(*c*) *Who's Who*, which gives brief biographical details of prominent people. (In addition, there is *Who Was Who*, providing a record of prominent people who have died.)

(*d*) *Kelly's Handbook to the Titled, Landed and Official Classes.*

8. Publications. Supposing it is wished to buy property in a certain area, or to insert advertisements in local papers in an area, then it is necessary to know about local newspapers in those areas. *Willing's Press Guide* is useful here.

For information about technical affairs in a particular trade, there are various trade journals, such as *Wool Record and Textile World*, *Grocers Gazette*, and so on.

9. Government reports. Copies of government reports and Acts of Parliament can be obtained from Her Majesty's Stationery Office in London or from its branches in large towns and cities in the provinces. For copies of government regulations, the various Ministries must also be contacted.

If copies of what was actually said in Parliament are required, then *Hansard*, published daily, must be obtained, again from H.M.S.O.

10. Companies and directorships. It is often necessary to obtain full information about a company and its directors, and here reference can be made to the *Stock Exchange Yearbook* and the *Directory of Directors*. Company information can also be obtained direct from the Registrar of Companies.

11. World place-names. When sending letters or parcels abroad, it is often useful to be able to refer to the country and the spelling of specific place-names. For this purpose, a good world atlas and a gazetteer would be useful.

12. Yearbooks. Some bodies publish a fresh book each year about a specific field, such as local government, the National Trust, etc.

13. General reference. *Pears Cyclopaedia* deals with a variety of subjects, including names of M.P.s, the royal family, prominent people, etc.

Whitaker's Almanack is also a most comprehensive reference book containing information on world affairs, statistical information about population, housing, etc., as well as sections on Nobel prizewinners, etc.

The *Medical Directory*, *Law List*, *Army List* and *Crockford's Clerical Directory* give information respectively about doctors, judges (also solicitors, barristers, etc.), army officers and clergymen.

14. Calculation. For the occasional calculations, it is useful also to have a good ready reckoner in the office (*see* XIX, **3**).

PROGRESS TEST 16

1. The only reference books in your general office are telephone directories. You are told that a sum of about £30 will be made available for the purchase of other reference books. Draw up a list of suggestions with reasons for each of your choices. [*R.S.A.*

2. (*a*) In what books of reference would you expect to find the following?

    Names and addresses of builders in the Manchester area.
    Details of the Datel service.
    Early closing day in Maidstone.
    First-class railway fare, London to Edinburgh.
    The meaning of F.R.C.S.
    Report of today's proceedings in Parliament.
    The population of Nairobi.

(*b*) Apart from reference books, name four other sources of information which are available to business. [*R.S.A.*

3. Name four books of reference which should be accessible in an office and say why you have chosen these books. [*U.L.C.I.*

XVI. BOOKS OF REFERENCE

4. What information can you find in (*a*) the *A.B.C. Railway Guide*, (*b*) classified telephone directory, (*c*) a dictionary, (*d*) *Whitaker's Almanack*. [*Y.C.F.E.*

5. Make a list of five reference books which would be useful in general office work. State the type of information to be found in each.
[*Y.C.F.E.*

6. Your buyer has to place an order for 25 2-m corrugated sheets of asbestos. Explain how he will locate and select a supplier. [*Y.C.F.E.*

7. The only books of reference in your office are telephone directories and a dictionary. Recommend six other reference books which may be purchased and state the uses of each. [*Y.C.F.E.*

8. What information can be obtained from:

(*a*) a classified telephone directory;
(*b*) *Stock Exchange Yearbook*;
(*c*) *Post Office Guide*;
(*d*) *Whitaker's Almanack*? (**4, 12, 13**)

9. From which reference books would you obtain the following information?

(*a*) The time taken for an air mail letter to reach Australia.
(*b*) The publisher and publication date of a popular monthly house magazine.
(*c*) The decorations of a well-known Member of Parliament.
(*d*) The verbatim report of a speech made in the House of Commons.
(*e*) The name and telephone number of a good hotel in Brighton.
(*f*) Information about the capital of a large public limited company.
(*g*) The telephone number of a coal merchant in a large city.
(*h*) The times of weekday trains from London to Nottingham.
[*E.M.E.U.*

10. In which reference books would you expect to find the following information?

(*a*) The names of the Lord Mayor of a particular city.
(*b*) The charges for bed and breakfast at the Royal Hotel, London.
(*c*) The first-class return fare to Manchester.
(*d*) The distance by road from Liverpool to London.
[*W.J.E.C.*

11. Give one item which may be found in *each* of the following reference books:
(*a*) *Whitaker's Almanack*.
(*b*) *Who's Who*.
(*c*) *A.A. Handbook*.
(*d*) The typist's desk book. [*W.J.E.C.*

CHAPTER XVII

PERSONNEL PRACTICE

1. Recruitment of staff. Most business concerns place advertisements in newspapers for the staff they require (although they also use private employment agencies, Careers Advisory Officers, etc.). In the advertisements, applicants are requested either to write a letter of application or to send for an official application form.

The reasons for the use of application forms are (*a*) it ensures that all the correct information is given and (*b*) it places such information in the same order on all applications, which makes it easier to compare one with another.

After the application letters or application forms are received, they have to be studied for the purpose of drawing up a "short list" for interview, usually about between six and ten of the applicants.

After the short list is drawn up, an interview is arranged, and usually either at the interview or subsequently the appointment is made.

Either before or shortly after the interview, references are followed up. It is the usual practice these days to ask for names and addresses of referees to whom application can be made direct for references about the character of the applicant.

2. Personnel matters. Usually, all personnel affairs are confidential, and even if not marked "confidential" they should go to the manager who maintains his own private files about his staff.

In a large company, the personnel officer maintains personnel records which contain staff details, such as the following:

(*a*) Name and address (and telephone number).
(*b*) Education and examinations passed.
(*c*) Date of commencement of employment.
(*d*) Wage or salary.
(*e*) Periods of sickness.
(*f*) Perhaps a timekeeping record and staff reports.

3. Conditions of service. Under the *Contracts of Employment Act* 1963, an employer is required to give every new employee (within thirteen weeks) a statement of his conditions of service.

This statement must include at least the following information:

(*a*) Identity of employer and employee.
(*b*) Date of commencement of employment.
(*c*) Normal hours of work.
(*d*) Rate of remuneration.
(*e*) Intervals at which it will be paid.
(*f*) Terms and conditions regarding holidays and holiday pay.
(*g*) Terms and conditions regarding sickness and sick pay.
(*h*) Terms and conditions regarding pension scheme (if any).
(*i*) Length of notice to be given by either side (*i.e.* by employer or by employee).
(*j*) Whether public holidays are paid for.
(*k*) If there is holiday pay entitlement on leaving, the method of calculation.
(*l*) The right to belong or not to belong to a trade union.
(*m*) Person to approach with a grievance, and details of the grievance procedure.

NOTE: There is no mention of what *work* is to be performed; this is purposely omitted because it may need to be changed. Neither is there any mention of overtime; usually contracts include a provision requiring such extra overtime as may be reasonably necessary from time to time.

(This Act, with amendments made by the *Redundancy Payments Act* and the *Industrial Relations Act*, is now consolidated in the *Contracts of Employment Act* 1972.)

4. Holidays. In most business concerns, annual holiday entitlement varies according to the grade of staff and the length of service in the business. Thus, where two weeks' holiday is normal, it may be expressed as one day's holiday pay for each month of completed service, so that to qualify for a full two weeks' holiday with pay it is necessary to have worked in the company for twelve months. If an employee has not qualified by length of service for full pay, some employers will allow the balance of holiday to be taken without pay.

5. Holiday rota. Some business firms have a holiday period (say April to September) during which all holidays must be taken. This is to avoid too much dislocation of staffing and work during the rest of the year.

With staff away on holiday, the management must ensure that the work of the office continues. To this end:

(*a*) holidays must be planned in advance;

(*b*) there must not be too many staff on holiday at the same time; and

(*c*) there must always be someone in the office who can deal with the work normally performed by another.

To satisfy (*a*), a holiday rota is prepared at the beginning of the year, and staff are requested to put down on the chart the holiday dates they would prefer. Usually, senior staff have first choice, followed by those with longer service with the company than others. Where there are a number of staff of equal status, holiday dates may present difficulties, and it may be arranged that the staff take it in turn to have first choice, or, alternatively, it may be settled by a ballot.

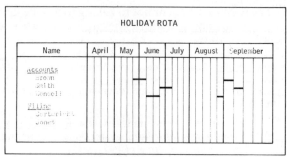

Fig. 24.—*Holiday rota.*

When all staff have put down their preferences, management has then to decide on problems arising from some members of staff wanting their holidays at the same time and draw up an official holiday rota. An example of this is shown in Fig. 24, and a copy is displayed in the department for staff to check and agree their holiday dates, as well as for making arrangements for the continuance of work in the absence of the holidaymakers.

6. Holidays in general. The purpose of holidays is that the staff may gain relaxation and improve their health, both physically and mentally, so that they can perform their duties more efficiently during the rest of the year.

Even if an employee cannot afford a holiday, employers may insist on one being taken, not only for the reasons stated above but also as a prevention against fraud. Any employee concerned with cash or stores should particularly be made to take a holiday, because it is when he is absent and another person is performing the duties that any fraud or misappropriation might be discovered.

It is also a way of ensuring that different members of staff are capable of performing the work of others, so that in the case of sickness substitutes of staff are possible. It is also a method of checking on performance of other jobs for the purpose of promotion.

PROGRESS TEST 17

1. (*a*) Why do many large business organisations ask prospective employees to fill in a printed "Application for employment" form?
 (*b*) What questions are likely to be asked on this form? (**1**)
 [*E.M.E.U.*

2. What are the office activities involved in the appointment of clerical staff? (**1**) [*N.C.T.E.C.*

3. (*a*) What is the purpose of keeping staff records?
 (*b*) Name three items of information which are usually found in the record of a member of staff. (**2**) [*Y.C.F.E.*

4. How should confidential and personal matters be dealt with in an office? (**2**) [*U.L.C.I.*

5. You are asked to produce a holiday rota for the ten members of your staff covering the months of June, July and August (a period of thirteen weeks). The staff consists of yourself and your assistant, one telephonist and a relief telephonist, typist, two general clerks, two shorthand typists, one copy typist and a junior trainee clerk. Each member of the staff is allowed to take two weeks' holiday. Draw up the necessary rota, ensuring that the department's work is adequately covered. (**5**) [*R.S.A.*

6. What rules should be followed when making up a holiday chart in an office? Draft a chart for fifteen employees, each of whom has three weeks' holiday, the holidays to be taken between May and September. (**5**) [*U.L.C.I.*

7. You are asked to prepare a holiday rota for the ten members of your staff covering the months of June, July and August (a period of thirteen weeks). Each member of your staff is entitled to two weeks'

holiday. The staff consists of yourself (in charge), your assistant (senior clerk), one telephone operator, a relief telephone operator-typist, two general clerks, two shorthand typists, one copy typist and a junior clerk.

 (a) State factors you would bear in mind in drawing up the rota.
 (b) Show the finished rota you would draw up. **(5)**   [*U.E.I.*

8. Why should staff holidays be enforced? Are there any particular employees for whom staff holidays should be enforced? **(6)**   [*U.L.C.I.*

CHAPTER XVIII

TIMEKEEPING AND WAGES

1. Time-recording. Different business concerns use different methods for recording time worked by their employees. The main methods are as follows:

(*a*) Time book: suitable and most usual for office staff (*see* **2** below).

(*b*) Autographic recorder: suitable for a small office staff (*see* **3** below).

(*c*) Time card recorder: most popular for factory workers (*see* **4** below).

2. Time book. Times may be recorded on a sheet of paper instead of in a book, but the rulings will be similar. The names of employees are listed down the left-hand side, opposite which are two columns, "IN" and "OUT", where the employees on arriving and leaving have to enter the times of arrival and finishing work.

Some business concerns have a special late book to avoid cheating, for this is the main disadvantage of a time book.

3. Autographic recorder. This is a machine fitted with a clock connected to a printing mechanism. On arriving, a worker depresses a lever on the machine, which opens a signature window over a roll of paper. The machine automatically prints the day and the time, and the worker signs his name against the printed time.

It is obviously more accurate than the time book, but its main disadvantage is that the names appear on the roll of paper in the order of arriving and not in pay number order.

4. Time card recorder. This is a machine fitted with a clock connected with a printing mechanism. Each side of the clock are racks marked "IN" and "OUT" which house the time cards.

A worker, on arriving, takes his card (identified by his pay number) from the OUT rack, places it in the clock which automatically prints the time on it, and then places the card in the IN rack. On going home, the employee reverses the process, placing his stamped card in the OUT rack.

This is really the best form of time recording, being automatic and giving an individual time record for each worker, which is very useful for wage purposes.

5. Methods of remuneration. Workers can be paid by either of the following methods:

(*a*) *Time rates*, by which wages are paid on the basis of either so much an hour (as in the factory) or so much a week, for the working of a standard week of so many hours.

(*b*) *Piecework*, by which wages are based on the amount of work performed; this is usual in a large number of factories.

A variation of this is the payment of a production bonus, by which, when work is completed in a shorter time than that scheduled, a special bonus is given based on the percentage of the time saved.

Overtime. In factories and in some offices, overtime is paid for at enhanced rates, *i.e.* the first two hours at time and a half, and subsequently at double time, on any single working day.

6. Methods of payment of wages and salaries. Wages and salaries can be paid in various ways:

(*a*) *In cash*. This is often used for paying factory workers.

(*b*) *By cheque*. This is usual for office workers and members of management.

(*c*) *By traders' credit*. This is usual for office workers in large business concerns, and is where cash is transferred direct to the workers' bank accounts. It is necessary for a worker to open a bank account if payment is made by this method.

7. Wages procedure. Wages systems will vary from one business to another, but the steps in a wages system will usually include the following:

(*a*) Giving every employee a pay number as a means of identification, to fix his position on the pay-roll, and as a means of prevention against fraud.

(*b*) The prior insertion on the pay-roll of all names and pay numbers.

(c) Checking on attendance and work records, according to whether wages are paid on a time or piecework basis. Where costing is involved (*i.e.* charging wages to different jobs) it is usual for workers to complete time sheets giving details of work performed, which must be counter-signed by their foreman.

(d) With this information, gross pay is calculated, *i.e.* wages free of deductions, which might be (say) 42 hours at 37p per hour.

(e) Entry of deductions from gross pay: National Insurance, P.A.Y.E., etc.

(f) Calculation of net pay, by taking all deductions away from gross pay.

(g) Entering of income tax on employees' tax records.

(h) Cash analysis, *i.e.* of the number of pound notes and different coins required.

(i) Drawing cash from the bank and putting cash in separate pay envelopes.

(j) Paying out wage envelopes to staff (identified by supervisor or on production of time card); some business concerns require a worker's signature on payment.

8. Adjustments to the pay-roll. Every week it is necessary to make adjustments to the weekly pay-roll for the following reasons:

(a) When an employee is sick, there arises the question of whether he is entitled to sick pay (entitlements usually vary according to length of service), and National Insurance should not be deducted in a full week of sickness. Therefore there must be some method of notification of employees off sick and those returning from sickness.

(b) When employees are going on holiday, there arises the question of entitlement to holiday pay, and if a person is going on (say) two weeks' holiday and is entitled to two weeks' holiday pay he will need to have two extra weeks' pay and have two extra weeks' deduction of National Insurance.

(c) Similarly, when an employee changes his job, has an increase in pay, or changes his income-tax code number, adjustments will have to be made.

(d) With factory workers, it is usual, as a penalty, to deduct perhaps a half hour's pay if the worker is more than three minutes late on any day. Therefore there has to be a system of notification of lateness of all employees.

9. Payment of Wages Act 1960. This Act legalised the payment of wages by two methods:

(a) By cheque or traders' credit, if the employee requests it in writing and the employer does not refuse.

(b) By postal order or money order (without request) when employees are absent through sickness or injury.

NOTE: This provision facilitates the payment of wages when an employee is sick, which previously presented many difficulties.

On taking up employment, if the conditions of service require payment of wages by cheque, then this is a condition of employment, and must be agreed to by the employee if he accepts the job.

10. Prevention of fraud in wages systems. Since the payment of wages usually involves large sums of money, it is advisable to initiate measures to prevent fraud, which may include the following:

(a) Divide duties (particularly the preparation of the pay-roll and paying out) between different members of staff.

(b) Institute internal checks, such as a periodic check with the National Insurance numbers.

(c) Internal audit, by which a surprise audit is carried out, perhaps at the time of paying out.

(d) To pay wages by cheque or traders' credit instead of in cash (this is one way of meeting the risk of pay-roll bandits).

(e) Have a definite system for dealing with unclaimed wages (*i.e.* employees absent on pay day); usually this is by a definite indication on the pay-roll and the checking and return of those pay packets to the company cashier.

(f) Have a periodical check with the staff records maintained by the personnel department.

11. National Insurance. An employer is under a statutory obligation to deduct National Insurance from every employee. The rates payable under the *Social Security Act* 1973 (which came into force on 6th April 1975) are $5\frac{1}{2}\%$ on all income over £11 a week up to £69, when it becomes a flat rate. The employer also has to pay $8\frac{1}{2}\%$ as his contribution, and the total deductions have then to be entered on the Deduction Card held for each employee for tax purposes.

Every month, the employer then pays the total of P.A.Y.E. and National Insurance deduction to his local Inspector of Taxes.

NOTE: Although N.I. cards are abolished for employed persons (Class 1), they will still be required for the self-employed (Class 2) and for those making voluntary contributions (Class 3).

12. National Insurance system. The office system consists of calculating the appropriate percentage of the employees' gross pay and entering it:

(*a*) on the pay-roll, and
(*b*) on the employees' Deduction Cards.

13. P.A.Y.E. (Pay As You Earn). This is a system of collecting tax from income as it is earned in the income-tax year, *i.e.* from 5th April. Each worker is given an income-tax code number which is related to his personal allowances (the amount he earns free of tax). Each week (or month) the employer calculates tax liability on the total pay in the income-tax year by using the code number for each worker and by reference to special income-tax tables provided by the Inland Revenue Department.

The most important forms are as follows:

(*a*) *P11* is the tax deduction card used for weekly and monthly deductions; a separate card has to be entered every week or month, showing pay and tax deducted therefrom for each employee.

(*b*) *P45* is a form in triplicate issued to an employee leaving a business. This shows details of his gross pay in the year, the tax deducted and his code number; the form should be signed by the employer.

The top copy is sent by the employer to the local Inspector of Taxes, and Parts II and III are given to the employee to take to his next employer, who sends one copy to his local Inspector of Taxes.

(*c*) If a new employee fails to produce a *P45* when he joins the company, the employer must send a *P46* form to the local Inspector of Taxes. *When an employee cannot produce a P45* (such as a new employee straight from school), then the employer will deduct tax in accordance with an emergency table and enter tax deducted on a *P14* emergency card. This means that tax is not deducted on the cumulative earnings in the year, but on a weekly basis, and except when an employee starts work on the 5th April it means that the employee is probably paying more tax than he should.

It therefore pays a new employee without a *P45* form to visit (or write to) his local Inspector of Taxes (in the area in which he works) requesting the appropriate form for the award of an income-tax code number.

(*d*) *P60* is the annual certificate of total pay in the year and tax deducted, and an employer is bound to give this form to every employee after the end of the income-tax year. It should be retained, not only for the possible increase of sick pay when an employee is sick subsequently, but also for the completion of an income-tax return which may be sent to the employee at the end of the income-tax year.

14. Employees joining or leaving. From the above, it is apparent that what must be sought from a new employee, and must be given to employees leaving, are the following:

(*a*) *P45* form, *i.e.* Parts II and III in each case.

(*b*) For an employee leaving, any wages due to the date of leaving. Whether holiday pay is due depends on the contract of employment, and whether holidays have been taken in the year. There is no automatic right to holiday pay, apart from specific provision in the contract of service, although most employers are fairly generous in this respect.

PROGRESS TEST 18

1. Describe *three* ways of timekeeping which would provide an adequate record for the calculation of time-rate wages. (**2, 3, 4**)

2. Write brief notes on *four* of the following in connection with wages; (*a*) time sheets, (*b*) overtime rates, (*c*) expenses, (*d*) holiday pay, (*e*) clock cards, (*f*) production bonus, (*g*) statutory deductions. (**5, 8, 11, 12**)

3. Describe the ways in which wages can be paid. What precautions should be observed? (**6, 10**) [*U.L.C.I.*

4. What information is required before the pay-roll can be produced for your firm's employees? (**7**) [*Y.C.F.E.*

XVIII. TIMEKEEPING AND WAGES 145

5. (*a*) Describe the step-by-step procedure when preparing the weekly pay-roll of a small manufacturing firm whose workpeople are paid on a day-rate basis. A certain amount of evening overtime is worked.

(*b*) Draw, with suitable headings, a wages schedule that would suit the above business. (**7**)

6. Draw up the headings of a firm's pay-roll sheet and enter up all the relevant entries in respect of an employee John Banks, for the week ending 15th June, using the following information:

42 hours worked at 40p per hour, including two hours' overtime at time and a half; income tax £1·10; National Insurance 92p; social club 1p; holiday club 50p. (**7**)

7. At the end of the pay-day, a wages clerk finds that he has not been able to pay an employee who is ill at home. What alternative means could he use to ensure that the employee receives his wages as soon as possible? (**9**)

8. Discuss how a system of internal check would operate in a large well-organised wages and accounts department. (**10**)

9. Describe a system for dealing with *unclaimed wages* within a business. (**10**) [*U.L.C.I.*

10. Explain what is meant by P.A.Y.E. Describe the office procedures for dealing with it, and give the function of any *two* official forms used. (**13**)

11. (*a*) You are working in the wages department of your company and you are told to complete a P45 for an employee leaving.

  (*i*) What information will you enter on it?
  (*ii*) Where will you get this information?
  (*iii*) What happens to the three parts of this form?

(*b*) You are also told to start an emergency card P14 for a new employee.

  (*i*) Why is this necessary?
  (*ii*) What effect is this likely to have on the amount of tax the employee will have to pay? (**13**) [*R.S.A.*

12. On joining your firm a new employee brings with him his income-tax form P45. Explain how you would deal with this form and what action you would take if an employee failed to produce it. (**13**)

[*Y.C.F.E.*

13. Describe the P.A.Y.E. system and give the functions of any *two* forms used in connection with P.A.Y.E. (**13**) [*U.L.C.I.*

14. When an employee leaves his employment what action must be taken by (*a*) the personnel department and (*b*) the wages department? Say what documents have to be completed and what becomes of them. (**14**) [*R.S.A.*

NOTE: The questions not followed by initials of examining bodies are suggested questions only.

CHAPTER XIX

ADDING, CALCULATING AND ACCOUNTING MACHINES

1. Types of machine.

(*a*) An *adding machine* is intended for addition and subtraction. It may be hand or electrically operated, and it usually has a tally-roll (on which the figures are printed), in which case it is called an "add-lister".

The first thing to do when using an adding machine is to clear the machine of any figures left in its internal workings by pressing the total key and then the power bar (or by pulling the crank if the machine is hand operated).

(*b*) A *calculating machine*, on the other hand, though it will also add and subtract, is primarily intended for multiplication and division. This type of machine is discussed in further detail below.

(*c*) An *accounting machine* is basically intended for posting (*i.e.* entering up) ledger accounts, although at the same time it will perform analysis. Some varieties of accounting machine are made specifically for the production of sales invoices and may be called "billing" or "invoicing" machines.

2. Types of keyboard. On all these machines three types of keyboard are obtainable, and the choice between them is one of the factors to take into account when buying a machine:

(*a*) *Full-bank*, having a number of vertical columns of figures numbered 1 to 9, according to the capacity of the machine.

(*b*) *Half-keyboard*, having vertical columns of keys numbered 1 to 5; when a number above 5 is required, then two consecutive key depressions are required (5 and 2 for 7, etc.).

(*c*) *Simplified keyboard*, where there are keys numbered 0 to 9 (sometimes there are separate "0" keys for one "0", two "0"s and three "0"s), and where the keys have to be depressed consecutively when entering an amount on the machine.

3. Other methods of calculation. Before a calculating machine is purchased, full consideration should be given to the following:

(*a*) *Ready reckoners* (books of tables), which are ideal where there is a small volume of calculations of a fairly simple nature.

(*b*) *Slide rules*, which are not usually used in the office for commercial calculations, but which are very useful to engineers, draughtsmen, surveyors, etc.

4. Calculating machines. The various types of calculating machine may be listed as follows:

(*a*) Key-driven calculators (*see* **5** below).
(*b*) Rotary calculators (*see* **6** below).
(*c*) Electric automatic calculators (*see* **7** below).
(*d*) Printing calculators (*see* **8** below).
(*e*) Electronic calculators (*see* **9** below).
(*f*) Electronic printing calculators (*see* **10** below).

The last three are modern developments of the last few years.

5. Key-driven calculator. With this type of machine a trained operator is employed, and calculations are performed by the quick depression of keys on the machine which automatically alter the figures shown in dials on the front of the machine. Multiplication is performed by repeated addition, and division by repeated subtraction. Such machines are very fast and would be advisable where a large volume of calculations justifies the employment of a full-time operator, but not for the occasional office calculation.

6. Rotary calculator. On this type of machine, the amounts are either set into the machine by levers round a barrel on the machine or key-set on a simplified keyboard. Calculations are then performed by turning a handle, clockwise for multiplication and anti-clockwise for division. It has a hand-operated carriage shift for moving the decimal place.

7. Electric automatic calculator. This machine is a development of the rotary calculator, but is powered by an electric motor. On depression of the appropriate keys, it will multiply and divide automatically; results show in dials on the machine.

8. Printing calculator. This machine has developed from an add-listing machine, usually with a simplified keyboard. Machines are available with double registers and a memory register. Calculations are performed by simply setting up the figures required and then pressing the appropriate multiplication or division key, when the answer is printed automatically on a tally-roll. It is electrically operated.

9. Electronic calculator. This is as simple to operate as a printing calculator, but instead of the figures being printed on a roll of paper they are displayed in neon lights in dials on the machine. The calculations are performed electronically and made literally in thousandths of a second; the machine is absolutely noiseless.

10. Electronic printing calculator. This is the most modern development and consists of a combination of the printing calculator and the electronic calculator; *i.e.* it performs calculations electronically, as well as giving a printed record of the figures used on a tally-roll.

11. Calculations in the office. The machines mentioned above vary in price from £10 to £500, and the machine chosen for an office will obviously depend on what the volume of calculations is likely to be, whether a trained operator is necessary, portability (*e.g.* if it is wished to move the machine from one desk to another), as well as the kind of calculation to be performed (*e.g.* simple invoice extensions or more complicated calculations involving square roots, etc.).

However, examples of work which calculating machines might be used for include the following:

    (*a*) Calculation of gross pay when preparing the pay-roll.
    (*b*) Extension of prices on sales invoices.
    (*c*) Checking extensions on purchase invoices.
    (*d*) Costing for cost accounting purposes.
    (*e*) Conversion into foreign currency.

XIX. ADDING, CALCULATING AND ACCOUNTING MACHINES 149

(*f*) National Insurance contributions.

(*g*) Calculation of investment income on shareholdings.

12. Central calculating department. As well as having central typing and perhaps central filing departments, there is a trend today towards having central calculating departments.

(*a*) *Advantages:*
  (*i*) Makes best use of calculating machines (which might be expensive).
  (*ii*) Trains experts in performing different calculations required.
  (*iii*) Avoids noise of having machines in different departments (although notice that an advantage of electronic calculators is their quietness in operation).
  (*iv*) Overcomes difficulty of absence of machine operators owing to sickness and holidays.

(*b*) *Disadvantages:*
  (*i*) Problem of communication between different departments and the central calculating department.
  (*ii*) May need special messenger system.
  (*iii*) Many offices need only occasional calculations and a machine provided locally may be more convenient.
  (*iv*) It may be difficult to fix responsibility, unless identifying rubber stamps are issued to the machine operators.

13. Writing boards (or "3 in 1" system). As an alternative to buying an accounting machine (*see* **14** below), a small business may choose to use a writing board (sometimes referred to as a "3 in 1" system), which consists of a hard plastic board with a clipping device. On this board are mounted three or more documents, *e.g.* the monthly statement, the sales ledger card and, thirdly, a summary of posting sheet.

By the insertion of carbon paper, it is thus possible to enter the three documents simultaneously by means of a ball pen. No calculations are automatically performed, but for this purpose one of the calculating machines listed above can be used.

The board is cheap to buy and simple to operate, and it does not require any special training of the operator.

14. Accounting machines. As mentioned previously, machines which can be grouped as accounting machines are sometimes called "book-keeping machines", "billing machines", etc. However, they all perform accounting work of the kind which is usually done in the accountant's department.

Basically, an accounting machine is used for Sales Ledger posting to customer accounts (the largest volume of paperwork in the accounts department). The three documents mentioned in **13** above are usually entered simultaneously, but the machine also adds or subtracts the figures entered at the same time. On the bigger, more expensive, machines multiplication is also performed automatically, as it is required for invoice extensions. The machine can also automatically calculate the new balance of account at each posting.

Some machines are fitted with a typewriter keyboard, whereby names and addresses of customers and details of goods can be typed on invoices and ledger cards.

Some have a programme bar (or plug-in programme tapes on expensive machines), so that the machine can automatically be converted from one use to another; this gives the machine greater flexibility in use.

15. Advantages and disadvantages of accounting machines.

(a) *Advantages:*

  (i) Saving in time and labour in posting.
  (ii) Greater legibility and neatness compared with handwriting.
  (iii) Greater accuracy (there are various methods of proof when using the machines).
  (iv) Automatic calculation and printing of the new account balance at each posting.
  (v) Simultaneous printing in one operation of the monthly statement, ledger card, summary sheet, etc.
  (vi) May perform analysis of sales, etc., at the same time as posting.

(b) *Disadvantages:*

  (i) If only one machine and one operator are employed, difficulties occur when the operator is sick or on holiday.
  (ii) Capital outlay on the machines, varying from £500 to £25,000.
  (iii) Disadvantages of having ledgers in loose-leaf form (individual ledger cards might be misfiled or mislaid).
  (iv) Sometimes there is lack of detail on the statements.

(*v*) Possibility of machine breakdown.
(*vi*) Noise in the office.
(*vii*) Difficulty of obtaining skilled, experienced operators.

16. Uses of accounting machines.

(*a*) Preparation of sales invoices, and perhaps monthly statements.
(*b*) Posting of sales ledger and summary sheet.
(*c*) Analysis of sales.
(*d*) Posting of purchases ledger and summary sheet.
(*e*) Posting of stock records.
(*f*) Posting of costing records.
(*g*) Preparation of pay-roll and tax records for each employee.
(*h*) For receipt writing (although note that where payments are received by cheque the current practice is not to issue receipts unless specially requested).

PROGRESS TEST 19

1. (*a*) Name the various mechanical and electrical aids that you would expect to find in the accounts department of a large company.
(*b*) What overall benefits would you assume that the company was getting from its mechanical aids? (**1, 15**) [*E.M.E.U.*
2. Give the advantages of using calculating machines in office work. (**1, 8, 9, 10**) [*U.L.C.I.*
3. Describe, briefly, some aids available to assist the calculations performed in a commercial office. (**3, 4**) [*Y.C.F.E.*
4. (*a*) What are the advantages of a simple book-keeping machine over a hand-posted ledger?
(*b*) For what purposes are rotary calculators used? (**11, 15**)
[*N.C.T.E.C.*
5. What services can be rendered to other departments of a medium-sized firm by a centralised calculating department which is equipped with key-driven machines? (**12**) [*E.M.E.U.*
6. Your firm, which is quite a small one, has been doing its accounts by hand. A salesman has tried to sell your employer a book-keeping machine with a small keyboard (*i.e.* ten or twelve keys). Another salesman has recommended using a "3 in 1" system on billing boards. Your employer asks you whether you know anything about either of these and requests that you write out notes for him stating how both types of equipment could be used. Set out your notes in the form of a simple report. (**13, 14**) [*R.S.A.*

7. Explain what is meant by the term "machine accounting". Give any advantages or disadvantages you know of this method. **(14, 15)**
[*Y.C.F.E.*

8. A medium-sized firm, still using pen and ink methods of book-keeping, is about to purchase an accounting machine. Briefly describe the types of work that could be carried out on this machine and discuss any advantages that might be derived from this installation. **(15, 16)**
[*E.M.E.U.*

CHAPTER XX

MISCELLANEOUS OFFICE MACHINES

1. Other machines in use. So far in this book, mention has been made of typewriters, dictating machines, photocopying and duplicating, adding, calculating and accounting machines, as well as franking machines used for outward mail.

Offices use a great number of machines today, and others commonly in use are:

(*a*) addressing machines: *see* **2, 3** below;
(*b*) punched-card machines: *see* **4, 5** below;
(*c*) computers: *see* **6-8** below;
(*d*) continuous stationery (although not a machine, it is used with various machines): *see* **9** below.

2. Addressing machines. These machines are used where it is wished to reproduce standing information at regular intervals, and to save the time and labour of fresh typing every time.

The standing information is put into:

(*a*) embossed metal plates;
(*b*) small stencils mounted on cardboard or plastic frames; or
(*c*) spirit masters mounted on cardboard or plastic frames.

Thus it is possible, after the master copies have been prepared, to reproduce the standing information from thousands of plates, etc., at a moment's notice. The machine saves time and labour in routine repetitive copying, and can be operated by fairly junior staff.

3. Uses of addressing machines. Addressing machines are very useful for the following:

(*a*) Initial preparation of the pay-roll (pay numbers and names).
(*b*) Printing names and addresses of customers on sales invoices and ledger cards.

(c) Printing on letters and envelopes which are sent to customers (*e.g.* when sending new price lists).

(d) Putting pay numbers and names on time cards.

(e) Preparation of index cards, *e.g.* of customers for credit control purposes.

(f) Printing dividend warrants when it is necessary to pay dividends to shareholders, once or twice a year.

4. Punched-card machines. These machines make use of standard sized manilla cards with vertical punching positions (0 to 9) in columns right across the card. Certain columns are allotted to each piece of information it is wished to put on the card and analyse.

(a) With the original data (say a copy sales invoice) in front of them, the punch operators then punch holes in the cards to represent the information relevant to each invoice (*punch*, hand or electric).

(b) The cards are then verified, or checked, by a senior operator to make certain they have been punched correctly (*verifier*).

(c) Then they are fed to a sorter which sorts out the cards (one column at a time) according to the analysis desired (*sorter*).

(d) Then the cards are fed to a *tabulator* which senses the holes punched in them and prints the interpreted information in tables (hence the name "tabulator") on paper and adds them up at the same time to give summary totals according to the analysis required.

5. Advantages of punched-card machines.

(a) Speed and economy of labour.

(b) More control information for management, obtained more quickly than previously.

(c) Sorting and tabulating, etc., are all performed automatically.

(d) They facilitate multiple analysis of the same information, *e.g.* analysis of sales by area, by product, by sales representative and so on.

6. Electronic computers. Electronic computers are being increasingly used in business, and, to describe them simply, they are machines which perform calculations at lightning speeds, which have "memories" that store figures, keep them up to date and put them back in the memory, and, lastly, which perform long sequences of operations automatically according to a programme fed into the machines.

Before a computer can be used, it is necessary first of all to employ a "*systems analyst*" who scientifically investigates the office systems and adapts them so that they can conveniently be processed by a computer. Secondly, the *programmer* writes out the programme of instructions by which the machine performs calculations on the figures fed into it.

A great deal of the success of a computer depends on the employment of properly trained systems analysts and programmers. In addition, there may be *punched-card operators* or punched-tape machine operators who put the information into machine language.

The basic parts of a computer (although not discernible on inspection) are as follows:

(*a*) Input (punched cards, punched tape, etc.).
(*b*) Arithmetic unit (which performs the calculations).
(*c*) Storage (or memory device—*see* above).
(*d*) Control (by the console and by the programmes fed into the machine).
(*e*) Output (punched cards, line-printer, teleprinter, etc.).

7. Advantages of computers.

(*a*) Great speed of operation.
(*b*) The production of control information not previously available to management.
(*c*) Greater accuracy of figures produced.
(*d*) Great flexibility in use (*see* below).
(*e*) Once the information is in machine language, all processing is automatic.
(*f*) Possibility of saving in labour and money costs.

8. Uses of a computer.

As mentioned above, an electronic computer is probably one of the most flexible machines used in office work, and the following applications are most popular (usually because they involve the greatest volume of routine clerical work):

(*a*) Preparation of the pay-roll, calculation of tax liability, production of statements of pay and cash analysis.

(b) Costing, *i.e.* the analysis of labour and material costs to different jobs, processes, etc.

(c) Stock controls, where the machine automatically compares stock levels with predetermined minima and reveals when reordering is required.

(d) Sales invoicing, where prices and product data can be held in the storage unit to be called on when required.

(e) Production planning, where material schedules and plant loadings are required for a factory.

(f) Market research, where analysis is made of all data collected; speed is often an important factor with this work.

9. Continuous stationery. Much of the speed of addressing machines, accounting and punched-card machines, as well as of computers, could not be obtained if it were not for the use of continuous stationery.

This is a device whereby office forms are printed in a long continuous strip, the forms being divided from one another by perforations. Usually a number of copies are obtained simultaneously.

In most cases the movement of the forms to the printing head of a machine is facilitated by the punching of sprocket holes down each side of the stationery, and its control of movement by sprockets which operate automatically.

The different copies of such continuous stationery are obtained by the use of the following materials:

(a) *One-time carbon.* This is thin, cheap, machine carbon interleaved by the manufacturer.

(b) *Carbon backing.* Here the deposit of carbon on the back of one form gives a carbon copy on the form beneath it. It is particularly useful where it is wished to copy only certain parts of the information.

(c) *Carbon pocket.* Here heavy carbons are placed between the copies in a set, and are used over and again until worn out.

(d) *N.C.R.* (*no carbon required*). The paper is impregnated with a chemical which automatically gives a carbon copy without the use of carbon paper at all.

PROGRESS TEST 20

1. Discuss in detail the use, and operation of, any one of the following:

    (a) Any type of duplicating machine.
    (b) Addressograph.
    (c) Guillotine.
    (d) Internal telephone system. (**2, 3**)   [*U.L.C.I.*

2. Describe the uses of an addressing machine, (b) a postal franking machine, (c) a stapler. (**2, 3**)   [*Y.C.F.E.*

3. Your company's statements of accounts are written out by hand at the end of each month. This results in a serious delay in posting them to customers. Suggest some modern methods which may help to expedite their preparation. (**2, 3**)   [*Y.C.F.E.*

4. In a punch-card system what are the functions of (a) punches and verifiers, (b) sorters, (c) tabulators? (**4, 5**)   [*U.L.C.I.*

5. What are the advantages of using punched-card machines in office work? (**4, 5**)   [*U.L.C.I.*

6. Describe two applications of the electronic computer to clerical work. What are the benefits of using a computer for these purposes? (**7, 8**)   [*E.M.E.U.*

7. Explain what is meant by "continuous stationery". For what purposes is it used and what are its advantages? (**9**)   [*E.M.E.U.*

8. Describe the work performed by *one* of the following: (a) adding-listing machine, (b) teleprinter, or (c) franking machine.   [*W.J.E.C.*

APPENDIX I

ACTS OF PARLIAMENT

THE student will find it useful to remember the main provisions of the following Acts of Parliament:

1. The Bills of Exchange Act 1882. Legislation relating to bills of exchange and cheques. It defines what is a bill of exchange and cheque, and the rights of parties to them.

2. The Partnership Act 1890. Lays down the law relating to businesses which are run in the form of partnerships (how many partners, rights of partners, etc.).

3. The Hire Purchase Act 1938. Relates to minimum deposits being paid and restricting seller's right to recover goods.

4. The Companies Act 1967. Main legislation about companies, their formation, management and dissolution.

5. Offices, Shops and Railway Premises Act 1963. Legislation for minimum physical conditions in the office (lighting, heating, ventilation, etc.).

6. Contracts of Employment Act 1972. Requires employers to give all new employees statements in writing of their conditions of service, and lays down minimum lengths of notice according to length of service.

7. The Hire Purchase Act 1964. Main requirements are that hire purchase agreements must disclose cash price as well as hire purchase price, and give hirer three days to cancel agreement.

8. The Transport Act 1968. Legislation for integration of nationalised road and rail freight services, and introducing new quantity licensing and restriction on transport drivers' working hours.

9. Social Security Act 1973. Revises previous National Insurance system by substituting total graduated payments instead of flat-rate and graduated contributions, and abolishing N.I. cards; but the self-employed pay both a flat rate and a new Class 4 percentage on gains or profits, and still have N.I. cards to stamp.

APPENDIX II
EXAMINATION TECHNIQUE

EXAMINATION hints are useless unless there has been a previous thorough study of the ground to be covered. But the author, from his experience of setting examinations and marking papers, always feels sorry for those students who fail for want of simple examination technique. The following general hints are therefore provided in the hope that students studying from this book will not fail on the grounds of faulty technique:

1. Read all the questions on the examination paper and decide which ones appeal to you. Attempt the easiest ones first; this gives you confidence.

2. Read the examination instructions and ensure that you follow them explicitly. Thus do not attempt more than the number of questions required (the extra answers will simply be crossed out by the examiner) and fasten your answers in numerical order.

3. For this purpose, write each question on a fresh piece of paper, for if you continue, say, Question 8 on the end of Question 1 you will not be able to assemble your answers in question order.

4. Write answers legibly on both sides of the paper.

5. Allot a certain amount of time per question according to the number of questions to be attempted and the examination time, and, if you have not finished a question in the time allotted, leave it and come back to it later if there is time available.

6. Do not write out the question. It only wastes time and is not necessary, for the examiner knows the questions.

7. To make sure the meaning of each question is absolutely clear, read it two or three times before putting pen to paper.

8. Think about your answer and jot down on a spare sheet of paper the points you wish to include in it; then start writing.

9. If the question is suitable, always enumerate your answer; *e.g.* list the advantages and disadvantages of a piece of equipment and number them 1, 2, 3, etc.

10. On the other hand, if the question asks for *a discussion* you should not enumerate but should instead write a discursive type of essay.

11. If a question requires more than one point in the answer, mark either on the examination paper or on your scrap paper the various points to be answered. If you attempt only half a question, the

maximum you can obtain will be half marks, and so make sure that you answer the whole question.

12. If you find that you are short of time, jot down on the answer paper brief notes of what you would have included in the answer; you will thus ensure some marks.

13. Write your answers in simple English and keep your paragraphs short. Nothing is more boring for the examiner to mark than a paragraph running the whole length of a page.

14. Questions requiring a factual answer, such as one on the legal position of hire purchase, must be answered by the statement of the facts required, and no amount of "padding", *i.e.* the statement of irrelevant material, will gain marks if the facts that are wanted are not stated. A short, concise and correct answer will gain more marks than a long, rambling one which evades the question. Answer the question, the whole question and nothing but the question.

15. If mistakes are made, do not alter the words but cross them through and write the correct version over the top of the mistake.

16. If time allows, read through all the answers before handing in your paper.

A model answer

Question. Describe the procedure you would follow before marking an invoice "good for payment" and explain why this is necessary.

Answer. The procedure on clearing a purchase invoice involves the following steps:

(*a*) Checking with the firm's official order, to ensure that the goods are of the quantity, the quality and price ordered.

(*b*) Checking with goods received notes, to ensure that the goods have in fact been received (a business does not want to pay for goods not received).

This is a most important step, and if there are any shortages, breakages, etc., these must be taken up with the supplier immediately, because the conditions of sale often state that claims must be made within three days of delivery. This makes it important that purchase invoices should be cleared daily.

(*c*) Checking the arithmetic on the invoice, *i.e.* the extensions and additions, in case there has been an arithmetical error in the calculation.

When all these checks have been carried out, and the invoice marked accordingly to signify each check, then it can be boldly marked, perhaps with a rubber stamp, "GOOD FOR PAYMENT".

This procedure is necessary and important because: (*a*) it is a method of helping to prevent fraud, *i.e.* dishonest employees putting invoices up for payment for goods not supplied; (*b*) it ensures that the company does not pay for goods not received or goods different from the kind ordered, or where invoices give higher prices than those quoted; (*c*) if the purchase invoices are cleared quickly, it may enable cash discount to be claimed for prompt settlement; and (*d*) the rubber stamping "GOOD FOR PAYMENT" makes it clear immediately that the invoice is *bona fide* and good for payment.

INDEX

A
A.B.C. Guide 129
Accountant, 8, 78
Accounting machines, 149
   advantages, 150
   disadvantages of, 150
Adding machines, 146
Addressing machine, uses of, 153
Address of titled people, 131
Advertising, 25
Air transport, 44
   advantages of, 45
   disadvantages of, 45
Air letters, 115
Alphabetical filing, 96
   rules for, 99
Annual stock-taking, 49
Audit, internal, 79
   professional, 79
Autographic recorder, 139

B
Bank, services, 59
Bank account, opening of, 60
Bank draft, 66
Bank statement, 71
Bill of lading, 34
Books of reference, 129
Business Reply system, 112
Buying, methods of, 15
   suppliers, 17

C
Calculating machines, 147
Calculations in the office, 148
c. and f., 46
Carriage forward, 41
Carriage paid, 41
Cash discount, 22
Cashier, 8
Cash in the post, 113
Central calculating, 149
Central filing, 100
Cheques, crossed, 63
   lost, 68
   marked, 66
   personal, 65
   post-dated, 69
   stale, 69
   travellers', 69
Chronological filing, 98
c.i.f., 46
Classification of filing, 96
c.o.d., 33, 115
Communications, 85
Company risk, 41
Company secretary, 7
Computers, 154
Conditions of service, 135
Consular invoice, 34
Continuous stationery, 156
Contracts of Employment Act 1963/1972, 135
Co-operative societies, 3
Costing, 8
Credit card, 68
Credit control, 26
Credit transfer, 66–7
Crossing, general, 64
   special, 65

Cross-reference, 95
Current account, 60
c.w.o., 33

D
Delivery note, 30
Departments, relationships of, 12
Deposit account, 60
Dictating machines, 121
Directors, 5
Dividend warrant, 66
Duplicating, offset lithography, 123
  spirit, 123
  stencil, 122
Dyeline copying, 125

E
Electric automatic calculating, 147
Electronic calculating, 148
Electronic computers, 154
  advantages of, 155
  uses of, 155
Electrostatic copying, 126
Export sales, 33
Express service, 113
Extended credit, 27
Ex works, 45

F
f.a.s., 46
Filing and records, 93
  equipment, 102
  systems, 93
f.o.b., 46
Follow-up (filing), 95
f.o.r., 46
Franco, 46

Franking machines, 111
Fraud, prevention of, 142
Freight Note, 44

G
Geographical filing, 97
Giro, National, 61

H
Hire purchase, 27
Holiday rota, 136

I
Imprest system, 76
Indexing, 101
Internal audit, 79
Invoice, sales, 31

K
Keyboard, 146
Key-driven calculators, 147

L
Letters, urgent, 113
Limited liability, 4
Local authorities, 3

M
Mail, inwards, 107
  outwards, 109
Microfilming, 103
Money and banking, 59
Money by post, 113
Monthly statement, 32

N
National Giro, 61
National Insurance, 142
Nationalised industries, 2

N.C.R., 156
Night safe, 59
Numerical filing, 97

O

Office functions, 82
    work, 83
Offset lithography, 123
Open cheque, 63
Order form, 20
Organisation, business, 6
Organisation chart, 7
Out guide, 94
Overseas post, 118
Owner's risk, 41

P

P.A.B.X., 85
Partnerships, 4
Pass book, 62
P.A.Y.E., 143
Paying-in book, 71
Payment, methods of, 61
Payments of Wages Act 1960, 142
Pay-roll, 141
Perpetual inventory, 49
Personal calls, 89
Personnel, 10, 134
Petty cash, 74
    book, 75
    vouchers, 77
Photocopying, 125
P.M.B.X., 85
Postal orders, 61
Post book, 110
Post Office Guide, 130
Printing calculator, 148
Private companies, 4
Private secretaries, 120
Public companies, 4

Public corporations, 5
Public relations, 25
Punched-card machines, 154
Purchases, routine, 79
Purchasing, 9

Q

Quotation buying, 18

R

Radio call systems, 91
Rail transport, 40
    charges, 40
R and D, 12
Recorded delivery, 114
Records, stock, 52–3
Recruitment of staff, 134
Reference books, 129
Refer to drawer, 69
Registered office, company's, 5
Registered post, 114
Remuneration, methods of, 140
Road transport, 36, 38
Rotary calculator, 147

S

Sales department, 24
Sales manager, 9
Sales procedure, 29
Shipping note, 43
Social services, 3
Sole trader, 4
Spirit duplicating, 123
Staff location, 91
Standing orders, 70
Statement, monthly, 32
S.T.D., 87
Stencil duplicating, 122

Stock, 48
   control, 48
   records, 52–3
   -taking, 49
   valuation, 52
Stores requisition, 55
Strip index, 102
Subject filing, 97

T

Telephone directories, 129
   etiquette, 87
   messages, 88
   operating, 86
   systems, 85
Teleprinter, 89
Telex, 90
Terms of payment, 21
Thermographic copying, 126
Three-in-one system, 149
Time card recorder, 139
Timekeeping, 139
T.M.O., 61
Trade discount, 21
Training, officer, 10
Transfer diffusion, 125

Transport Act 1968, 37
Transport, air, 44
   road, 36
   sea, 42
Travellers' cheques, 69
Typewriters, 119
Typing pool, 120

U

Urgent letters, 113

V

Valuation, stock issues, 55
Value Added Tax, 33
Visible card index, 101

W

Wages, methods of payment, 140
   procedure, 140
Wall charts, 104
Welfare officer, 10
Wheel index, 101
Window envelopes, 115
Works manager, 11
Writing boards, 149